Early Trains

Bryan Morgan

Camden House Books

Camden House Books
Printed and published by BPCC Publishers
Manufactured under licence from the proprietor

Created, designed and produced by
Trewin Copplestone Publishing Ltd, London

Made and printed in Great Britain by
Purnell and Sons (Book Production) Ltd.,
Member of the BPCC Group, Paulton, Bristol

ISBN 0 905015 04 5

The author would like to express his thanks
for the help given by Alan Jackson and
John Snell

Acknowledgments

The photographs for this book were taken by Geremy
Butler except those credited below to:
Baltimore & Ohio Railroad Company: 70/71;
Barnaby's Picture Library, London: 16; British Rail:
31, 34, 54, 54/55, 67b; Delaware & Hudson Railroad
Corporation: 18; Erie Railroad: 71tr; Ferrovia dello
Stato, Rome: 59t; Howard Loxton: 4b, 5, 19, 22/23,
32t, b, 46, 55, 58t, 59b, 60, 61t, b, 64bl, 69bl, 71tr,
72/73b; Mansell Collection: 72/73t, 77, 80t; Radio
Times Hulton Picture Library: 14t, 26, 28, 30, 38,
43b, 58b, 66l, 66/67, 69br, 70t, 71tl, 76t; Union
Pacific Railroad: 72/73b, 74/75t, b, 78l, 78/79, 80b.

The publishers also gratefully acknowledge:
The Museum of British Transport: 1, 6/7, 8/9, 13t,
17t, 20, 21t, b, 24/25t, b, 29b, 33t, 35, 36, 37, 40t, 41t,
b, 43t, 44t, b, 45t, b, 47t, 48bl, br, 52t, b, 53, 56, 57t,
64t, br, 65, 68t, b, 69t; Illustrated London News: 17bl,
br, 33b, 39, 42, 62; Science Museum, London: 7r, 8tl,
tr, 9r, 10/11, 12, 13b, 15, 27t, b, 29t, 37b, 40b, 48t,
50t, c, b, 57b.

Contents

Page 1
*The Stockton & Darlington railroad, opened on
27 September, 1825.*

The Dawn of Railroads

GROOVED into some paving slabs on the island of Malta are a series of parallel ruts adapted for the passage of wheeled vehicles or, perhaps, sledges. These are not unique survivors, for similar tracks have been found dating back to the Homeric age in Greece. But they are the earliest, being believed to date back to about 2000 BC.

At a glance they seem to have little enough to do with railroads. In the first place they are ruts, and a sunken rut is surely the very reverse of a raised rail. And, secondly, it is not always clear whether such ways were deliberately planned or whether they arose spontaneously from the tendency of a cart to slip into the shallow grooves made by one which had passed earlier, a habit which must have struck the builders of the Pyramids as they hauled their sleds across yielding sand. But they have one factor in common with the railroad proper in that they provide the elements of guidance and the reduction of friction.

In time, the true railroad was to add its own gifts of speed, safety, high capacity and much more. But these two advantages—that it needs no steersman, and that it makes good use of its propulsive power—link it back to the Pharaohs of 5000 years ago.

After the collapse of the Roman empire there is little evidence for more than a millenium of anything related to a railroad. It is perhaps hard to imagine Europe's great mediaeval cathedrals and castles (or the temples of the Incas) being built without the aid of temporary conveyors, and one stained glass window of about 1350 shows something of this kind. But the incentive towards radical new developments did not come until the sixteenth century.

From 1520 onwards, though, there appear hints of the discovery that—particularly in bad weather—a wheel running on a narrow raised rail presented as little as one tenth the resistance to motion as did a conventional wide cartwheel on a rough road. Unless some form of flange or protective flat rim was incorporated in either wheel or rail the wagon would of course slip off and so the other characteristic of railroads, that of guidance, was provided too. So important was this second factor in narrow tunnels that on one system ordinary tubs were guided by pins working in slots.

It is still a matter for debate whether the credit for these simple **tramways**—in which wheels and rails alike were of soft timber—should go to Silesia, Alsace or some land between the two. What is certain is that, if only through their intimate connexion with mining, the tramways were often associated with inclined planes—and that by the close of the sixteenth century such brief precursors of the railroad were no longer innovations on the continent of Europe.

Britain's own mineral wealth lay largely in the form of coal, the extraction of which was to increase tenfold in the seventeenth century; and here the "rayle" way appeared around 1600. It is probable that the innovation came over with the European experts who were invited by Elizabeth I to revitalize Britain's mines, but the first recorded step was a purely local one in that it was due to Huntingdon Beaumont, a colliery owner credited with "many new and extraordinary inventions and practices" who was one of the first of a new breed of capitalist entrepreneurs. For (probably in 1603, the year of the queen's death) Beaumont opened a two-mile run of inclined tracks to serve his mines at Wollaton, near Nottingham.

Soon there were developments in another of the forcing-grounds of the industrial revolution, the mining area of Shropshire around Coalbrookdale. Later Beaumont himself built a longer system in Northumberland in the area which was to become the cradle of all Britain's railroads. By the middle of the seventeenth century an extensive network was growing up on either bank of the lower Tyne and was attracting the foreign visitors who referred to such early lines as "Newcastle roads"—for Britain had now firmly seized the world lead in industrial inventiveness. Thus, the tramways of County Durham have the distinction of having bequeathed what is beyond doubt the world's earliest railroad relic, an embankment dating from 1663.

Nearby, though sixty years later in its construction, is an equally noteworthy memorial—the fine bridge in the form of a semi-circle with a diameter of over 100 feet, known as the Causey arch, built by a local mason. But by 1730 tramways themselves had ceased to be remarkable and could be found from South Wales to the Scottish Lowlands, where the earthworks of a track passing near Prestonpans played a part in that historic battle of the 1745 Jacobite rising. Another noteworthy line (and the first instance of a tramway not built in connection with coal-mining) was constructed to carry stone for Ralph Allen's rebuilding of the city of Bath.

worked tracks. The whole story of the innovation is complex and incomplete, but an important part in the coming of iron rails was certainly played by the Shropshire works (described by a contemporary as a "very responsible and opulent company") founded by Abraham Darby, a Quaker who had been one of the pioneers of the use of coke in smelting.

Edgeways and Plateways

THE Shropshire rails were of simple rectangular section, and engaged with pulley-shaped wheels. This was to prove a model for many lines built in northern England in the last years of the eighteenth century – those years which also saw the appearance of America's first tramways. But in South Wales, which was now entering a period of rapid industrial development, lines of a different pattern had become popular before 1800. It is worth noting that it was probably in Wales that the term tramway for a light, industrial, horse-hauled railway first became current, for the term derives from an old stem meaning "to draw" and was in use well before the time of the engineer Benjamin Outram. The legend that railroad points or switches with moveable

Wood or Iron?

THE first European tramways were built entirely of timber, with the running rails mounted on underframes of **sleepers** which for the more ambitious lines were set in gravel ballast. A wide variety of gauges was used, varying from under 2 feet up to 5 feet or more.

Yet, for all their cheapness and ease of replacement, wooden rails and wheels had grave disadvantages. They were poor frictionally, for example, and were short-lived due to their softness, inflammability and susceptibility to rotting. The first improvement, made about 1725, was to face the wheels themselves with wrought iron tires. However, these naturally imposed heavy wear on the timber rails and so, after experiments with various hardwood facings, engineers began before 1750 to plate at least the more heavily-used sections of their tracks with thin strips of metal.

Finally, from the 1770s onward, newly laid lines began to use all-iron rails, a later improvement being to mount these in **chairs**. Wooden rails, however, long endured on lightly

tongues were first devised by a Welsh miner sketching in the dust of his chapel during an interminable sermon is, however, only a legend.

In the Welsh system the wagons themselves had plain wheels and the flanges were incorporated into the rails or **plateways** from which derived the term **platelayer** still current in Britain. These rails, like those of the simpler **edgeways**, were themselves normally of cast rather than wrought iron, were correspondingly brittle, and came in very short lengths. Almost every maker had his own pattern, and with the problem of local gauges added it is not surprising that through-working between different systems was rarely possible.

Despite the pleas of such far-seeing men as Benjamin Outram in favor of national norms, Britain's railroad were beginning with a typical lack of standardization. But they were at least beginning, and around the close of the eighteenth century systems were set up which were not mere canal feeders or inter-works facilities: soon, for instance, lines of twenty miles or more were to be found. An increasing proliferation of different types of rail was in use,

certainly, and most of them were rather unsatisfactory, if only because the habit of spiking rails of cast iron down on to unyielding granite blocks led to frequent breakages. But after the introduction of fairly long sections of rolled iron early in the nineteenth century matters improved, and in any case such circumstances seemed to men of vision mere details in comparison with the fact that the tramways, like the canals, were now less exclusively tied to heavy minerals: they were carrying varied freight and playing an increasing part in the expanding economy of an urbanized and industrialized land. Might not such tramways, then, be one day welded into a nation-spanning system employing mechanical power?

Visions of Power

AS early as 1712 men could watch the world's first steam engine at work. For steam power is considerably older than James Watt and his apocryphal kettle: the technique

of boiling water in one vessel and of admitting the resulting vapor into another in controlled puffs arose when the needs of mining engineers for continuously working drainage pumps could be satisfied by the products of a sufficiently sophisticated metal-working industry. This technique was first introduced in Staffordshire – but the name connected with the innovation is that of Thomas Newcomen, an engineer from the mines of Cornwall who built on the work of Thomas Savery to give the world its first reliable source of artificial power.

Newcomen's engine, though, did not use its steam directly. Instead, it relied on the force of the atmosphere acting after each injection of vapor had condensed to water again and thus left a partial vacuum. And so it was left to James Watt, working towards the end of the century, to devise a pumping engine which – though it outwardly resembled Newcomen's with its great rocking beam – operated on the better principle of using the force of the steam itself. After it had done its work, this steam returned to the liquid state in a third vessel or external condenser, a technique which not only added to the pressure difference between the supply and exhaust sides of the cylinder but allowed the engine to work at an economically high temperature.

Watt made other improvements to the steam engine, all of which helped it to run steadily and automatically. But even his machines worked at very low pressures. This was perhaps inevitable in a period when boilers were little more than enlarged kitchen "coppers," when cylinders were adopted from the artilleryman's cannon, and when the fitter was lucky if he achieved a circularity of his bore, and a fit of his piston, accurate to much better than $\frac{1}{4}$ inch. Yet it meant that, as a power generator, the Watt engine was grossly inefficient in terms of both its expensive bulk and its fuel consumption.

This did not matter unduly for a stationary pit-head engine, but it did mean that (as Watt himself realized) such machines were quite unsuited to bring power to where it was most needed – the world of transport, where the water-wheel which could provide an acceptable substitute for the steam engine in mill or factory was inapplicable. It was, indeed, largely because of the bulk of early steam engines that their first practical transport use was in shipping. At least two eighteenth-century experiments with steam propulsion on the roads (by Joseph Cugnot in France in 1769 and by Watt's rebellious pupil William

Murdoch in 1784) showed promise, but technology had not yet progressed far enough along the way towards a compact, high-pressure engine for them to be wholly successful.

Early road locomotives also met with opposition both from the huge vested interest in horse-drawn carriages and from a public which regarded them as inventions of the devil. This suggests one reason why the "locomotive" engine was to be first developed on rails rather than roads: private tracks were comparatively safe from those who, for various reasons, feared and attacked the fiery monsters. But as yet even the rails were not quite ready for an invasion by steam. That came, fittingly, at the dawn of the new century.

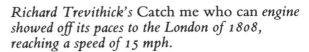
Richard Trevithick's Catch me who can *engine showed off its paces to the London of 1808, reaching a speed of 15 mph.*

Trevithick and his Locomotives

THE late 1700s had seen two developments with apparently little in common. One was a steady improvement in techniques for casting, assembling and machining metal components. The other was a theoretical examination which laid the foundations of the science of thermodynamics and which suggested that an efficient engine need admit only a small amount of high pressure steam and then let it do most of its work by expansion.

These advances turned men's minds towards the possibilities of a type of steam-powered engine which would work at a high enough pressure to allow it to dispense with its heavy

condenser. And outstanding among those who accepted this challenge was another Cornish engineer, the Celtic and temperamental Richard Trevithick.

Beginning with models and moving on to a prototype, Trevithick eventually succeeded in producing a road locomotive which, on the Christmas Eve of 1801, hauled a party of seven or eight enthusiasts who hung on as best they could while it steamed up a steep hill. A later road vehicle made successful trips in London at up to 10 mph. Trevithick was then invited to build an engine for a tramway at Pen-y-Darran in South Wales.

This locomotive, with its single vertical cylinder, 8-foot flywheel and long piston-rod whistling past the driver's ear like a trombone slide, was still a crude affair. But it employed the very important principle of turning the exhaust steam up the chimney, so producing a draft which drew the hot gases from the fire more energetically through the boiler.

So, on 21 February, 1804, the world's first steam train ran, triumphantly covering a course of less than 10 miles downhill in a leisurely four hours. Trevithick went on to display an improved engine–the well-advertised *Catch me who can* – on a circular track in London. But after this demonstration had been interrupted by the breaking of a rail, Trevithick seems to have lost interest in locomotion; instead he wasted in South American mining ventures what little capital he had accumulated, and died a disappointed man.

Richard Trevithick (1771–1833), Cornwall's pioneer of the horseless carriage on road and rail.

A prospect of Middleton colliery near Leeds and of one of John Blenkinsop's rack-aided locomotives built for Matthew Murray's line there.

Another reminder of Trevithick's demonstration—a souvenir ticket kept by one of the daring sightseers who traveled behind Catch me who can

Tracks and Traction

THE broken rail which put an end to Trevithick's London demonstration was more than a casual hazard. It was typical of one of the major problems which the engineers of the first decade of the nineteenth century encountered in their attempt to put steam to work on the tramways. This problem was that neither satisfactory rails nor well-sprung rolling stock had as yet been devised, so that fractures and derailments were everyday events.

Another hazard of the period existed mainly in the minds of the pioneers, but it proved equally influential. This was the belief that a locomotive with smooth wheels working on smooth rails could never, however great its tractive effort, provide the adhesion necessary to get a heavy load moving or haul it up the gentlest of gradients. Hence arose some experiments with weird engines which walked on legs or crawled along ropes.

It might be thought that the idea had

been opened to link the Thames to limestone quarries deep in Surrey. Though it used only animal power, this line has several claims to fame, including the Act of Parliament by which it became a general freight transporter or **common carrier,** an enterprise in its own right rather than the adjunct of some other industry and hence a stage closer to the present concept of a railroad. But an equally important development was that the threat of Napoleon's interference with shipping in the English Channel soon led to a survey designed to prolong the line all the way from London to Portsmouth.

Another advance came in 1804 when a tramway from Swansea acquired powers to run a regular passenger service. Shortly afterwards, a humble little span in Wales could claim to be the first metal rail bridge. Piece by piece the railroad jigsaw was taking shape.

Puffing Billy and Others

NAPOLEON'S threat to invade England never became a reality. But one side-effect of the wars with France transformed Britain's transport situation. By increasing the price of animal fodder, they added greatly to the appeal of powered traction.

already been exploded by experience, though it should be remembered that the weakness of the tracks of the age meant that designers had to use very light locomotives: with a load of only a few tons bearing on their two or three axles these naturally lacked much "bite" on the rails. But this fallacious belief over-shadowed the next historic experiment – the bringing of steam traction to the Middleton line near Leeds. For though the locomotives which John Blenkinsop designed for this occasion in 1812 incorporated such improvements as the use of twin cylinders, their builder did not trust them to work their way ahead without cog-toothed driving wheels which engaged with a rack-way laid beside one rail.

Meanwhile, as engineers struggled with their local problems, there were still the far-sighted who dreamed of railroads which would network Britain in the same fashion as did her canals. At the beginning of the century, for instance, a plateway built by the contractor responsible for the old London Bridge had

A detail of Puffing Billy. *The power from twin vertical cylinders was transmitted to a central lay-shaft and thence to the driving wheels by means of the gearing shown.*

Another generation was to pass before the economic balance was seen to be firmly in favor of the "iron horse", but in the second decade of the nineteenth century a new urgency was lent to the quest for a satisfactory steam locomotive–and, equally, for track which would not break almost daily. The latter came with the production of fairly long rolled rails of reliable quality. When mounted on resilient wooden sleepers these did not need the various types of stiffening which had been employed with the older forms, and though they themselves were made to diverse patterns there was a move towards a simple I-shaped section. Certainly after about 1810 the plateway was doomed.

As to the locomotive, several experimental models followed Blenkinsop's pioneers: these had more or less success, but even the best of them did not use his rack system and one even incorporated a **bogie** or wheels set on a swiveling truck to lead the engine around bends. There is no doubt, however, that the the most important work was done on the five-mile line at Wylam in Northumberland.

Here the colliery owner, Christopher Blackett, was a firm believer in the possibilities of steam traction; and so he asked his manager, William Hedley, to carry out experiments which would once and for all settle the question of adhesion. Hedley did so with the aid of a primitive **dynamometer car** to measure his engine's performance, and showed that racks and similar devices were quite unnecessary. Around 1814 he then went on to build a group of three locomotives which, though incorporating only one major technical advance (the use of a pattern of valve which allowed steam to work on both sides of the piston), were so soundly engineered that they ran for nearly fifty years.

Even then their story did not end, for in 1862 it was appreciated that these Wylam engines had set the seal of reliability on the steam locomotive. Two of them were therefore preserved for posterity and today form by far the world's earliest such survivors–*Wylam Dilly* in Edinburgh, and the immortal *Puffing Billy* in London. And now the scene was set for the appearance of one of its greatest actors.

A general view of William Hedley's immortal Puffing Billy.

Stephenson the Elder

GEORGE Stephenson was over thirty years old when he first became involved with his time's most pressing technical problem, having spent his apprentice years first in self-education and then in designing miscellaneous mining machinery. Not until 1813 was he asked by his employers to produce an engine for another Northumberland colliery, Killingworth.

This engine (named the *Blücher* as a compliment to Britain's ally in the war against Napoleon) was essentially a copy of Blenkinsop's without the rack. Although it was the first to run on a normal edgeway it, like its contemporaries, incorporated few novel features. But as a decade passed Stephenson made one improvement after another. Thus, an ingenious system of steam springs, in which the axles bore on pistons working in small cylinders, bridged the gap until the coming of reliable metal springs about 1820, and driving wheels were coupled together with rigid rods.

Another important advance of the time was the move away from a single flue carrying the hot gases from the firegrate, and towards passing these gases through a system of dozens of small fire-tubes. This was a great improvement over the old method, in which the flue was at most doubled or bent back in U form to offer a larger surface to the surrounding water. Several engineers made progress here, though, and even the final improvement of the period was not entirely Stephenson's own.

This was the first step towards an arrangement of eccentrics, rods and valves by which a single lever could smoothly control the **cut-off** of the locomotive–the amount of steam admitted at each stroke, which gave an alternative method of power-control to the use of the throttle–and then, after passing through a neutral position, could offer a reverse range. Although the principle of the variable cut-off dated from the days of stationary engines, reversal had been such a problem with early locomotives that some had to be adjusted while stopped and others could not run backwards at all. George Stephenson's gearing (which in fact owed much to his colleague, the ingenious and experimentally minded Nicholas Wood) marked an important stage in the quest for simple, reliable and precise control over both cut-off and reversing, and after it had been perfected it was, despite its weakness at high speeds, used on many locomotives until the final days of steam power.

Railroad Rivals

ALTHOUGH by 1820 the "traveling engine" was established as a reliable source of power for colliery use, there followed one of the curious hiatuses which mark the early story of railroad development. This lack of interest is illustrated by the fact that at the time George Stephenson himself was the only person in the world regularly building locomotives, and that even he considered them a comparative side-interest in a career which included the invention of the safety lamp and, as his first major venture into civil engineering, the laying of a well-engineered colliery tramway.

Some of the reasons for this delay were economic and political, but there were technical ones too. In the first place, not only were waterways still carrying the bulk of long-distance goods but engineers such as Thomas Telford had so improved some of Britain's major roads that passenger transport, though

very expensive, was faster and more comfortable than of old. (There were, for instance, merchants who commuted daily from Brighton to the City of London during the brief heyday of the stage-coach between 1820 and 1840). Telford even had a scheme to reserve tracks on these roads for steam engines, and it is interesting to speculate whether, if the highways of the Regency age had been a little better and public money more freely available, the railroad would ever have become more than a works facility. Another of the great "ifs" to consider is how far the tramways could have developd had steam not come to their aid.

A further reason for the comparatively slow development of the modern railroad is that many observers were still not convinced that the locomotive offered the best use of steam power for haulage. Thus, boiler explosions were not unknown with high-pressure mobile engines, in contrast to the safety of the stationary engine which now had over a century of use behind it. The most obvious transport employment of the fixed engine was, of course, to power a cable-incline, and só well did it do this work that many tramways with a steady, steep gradient were later re-aligned so as to consist of almost level stretches broken by very sharp climbs. Considerable ingenuity was often shown in these layouts, so that, for example, a pair of planes might be coupled to allow a tramway to negotiate a hump with the maximum of assistance from gravity. Inclines were also included in a number of otherwise conventional railroads built much later, and in some cases remained in use until quite recent years.

"Balanced" cable inclines at Brusselton, on the northern section of the Stockton & Darlington line. The winding-house design has typical echoes of Regency elegance.

An example of incline-building on the grand scale was afforded by the 30-mile Cromford and High Peak line. Opened in 1825 and linking the Manchester area to the south-east over a high, dry massif, this was one of the last, and certainly the most ambitious, of all tramways. It was designed for horse haulage and was laid out like a canal with a number of short, straight sections linked by curves of a radius too tight to be rounded at more than a walking pace; but such works as its tunnels were substantially built, and so too were the great inclines up which stationary engines hauled their wagons for limestone.

From Stockton to Darlington

IN the early 1820s there appeared on the British railroad scene one of those non-conformists who played so large a part in the Industrial Revolution. This was Edward Pease, who needed to bring coal down from pits near Bishop Auckland in County Durham to Darlington and to Stockton-on-Tees.

It is typical of this age of transition that Pease should have considered building a canal, and that what eventuated (though the fact is concealed by the immortal name of a line which has seen 150 years of continuous service) was in essence a two-part system. From the coalfields for some 15 miles down to Darlington it was a tramway, using horse haulage, inclines and—since timber ties became damaged by the hoofs of horses—stone sleeper-blocks. But a tramway itself could by now be a well-engineered concern, perhaps with a right of way nearly 20 feet wide boasting double tracks and with its gradients so controlled by substantial earthworks that a single horse could haul 50 tons uphill—and then, if the engineer had been careful to include no counter-gradients, hitch a lift down again in a special "dandy" wagon. And over the 12 miles between the eponymous towns of the Stockton and Darlington still more substantial rails were laid and even more money invested in ensuring a level roadbed.

Here too, though, a mixture of track materials was employed, and the question of the system of traction to be used was itself left open for some while after 1823. This was the year when Edward Pease appointed as his chief engineer the one man in the world best qualified to advise on both the civil and the mechanical fronts, George Stephenson.

Below *Contestants at the Rainhill trials, held in 1829. The second strip from the top shows all four contestants.*

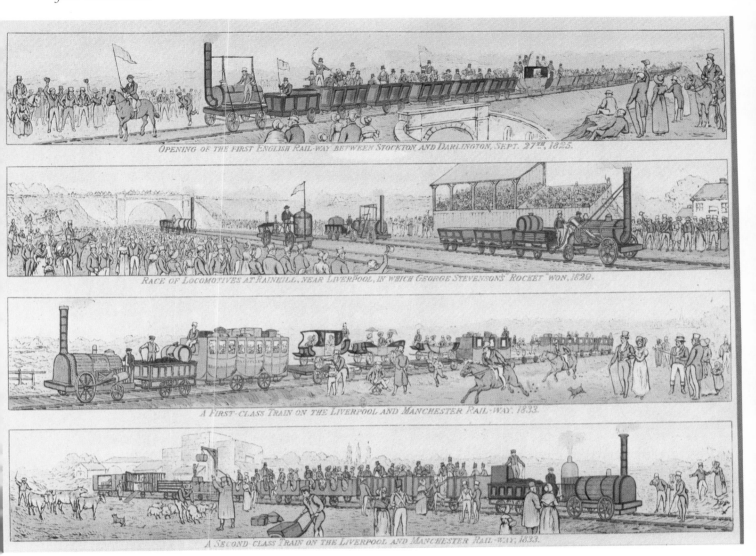

OPENING OF THE FIRST ENGLISH RAIL-WAY BETWEEN STOCKTON AND DARLINGTON, SEPT. 27TH, 1825.

RACE OF LOCOMOTIVES AT RAINHILL, NEAR LIVERPOOL, IN WHICH GEORGE STEVENSON'S ROCKET WON, 1829.

A FIRST-CLASS TRAIN ON THE LIVERPOOL AND MANCHESTER RAIL-WAY, 1833.

A SECOND-CLASS TRAIN ON THE LIVERPOOL AND MANCHESTER RAIL-WAY, 1833.

A Great Public Way

GEORGE Stephenson now had the assistance of his son Robert. Together, the two surveyed with their home-made theodolite the muddy miles from Stockton to Darlington and up into the coal-fields, perhaps meeting Pease over a bottle of claret in the evenings to discuss the day's work. Pease himself demanded the best the age could produce for, as he told George Stephenson, "In making the survey it must be borne in mind that this is for a great public way". But at last he was satisfied, and on September 27, 1825, traffic began on the Stockton and Darlington railroad.

There is one claim which can be made without doubt for the S & D—that it was the world's first fully public line in the sense that from the start it was empowered by Parliament to carry not only all forms of

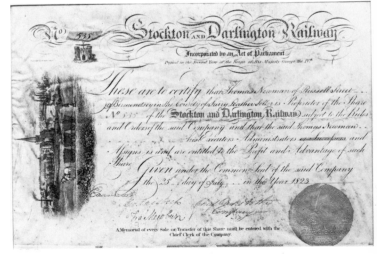

Stockton & Darlington share certificates, issued in 1823, suggested that motive power would be provided by superior horses rather than by steam locomotives whose use had in fact been authorized some months earlier.

13

The first locomotive of the Stockton & Darlington railroad hauling a replica train for the centenary of 1925.

freight but passengers too. Indeed, independent hauliers were allowed to work their own carriages over its metals. It also operated (as a subsidiary interest of the Stephensons) a plant which built the locomotives which, George Stephenson insisted, should handle freight traffic on the lower section. One of its bridges was the first railroad structure ever to be designed by a professional architect, and the system even had a passenger station of sorts though this was merely a converted cottage at a level crossing. Passengers admiring these novel features might be pardoned for treating as an engineering detail the fact that the gauge adopted for the S & D, as for most lines built since about 1815, was an arbitrary 4 feet 8½ inches or so. Whatever the ultimate origin of this figure (and it remains a subject for debate among experts), it had been adopted by Stephenson for his colliery tramways and seemed to work well enough for the transport of passengers as well as of freight. Certainly in 1825 none foresaw that a width which had been hit on almost accidentally in the coal-fields of Northumberland was destined to become one of the world's great standards.

Despite these progressive pointers, however, the S & D was not yet ready for the final step

of hauling the general public behind steam. The locomotives' work was restricted to handling coal, and for many years ordinary passengers continued to travel in horse-hauled wagons.

Passengers – up to 600 of them, as well as a heavy load of freight – were, however, carried on the inaugural train which, as those who raced it on foot or horseback could confirm, traveled at some 12 mph behind another classic preserved engine. Called at first *Active*, but later simply *Locomotion*, this was essentially a copy of Stephenson's colliery locomotives. Three sisters of its type were built and, despite the usual explosions and some difficulties caused by the fact that the S & D was considerably longer than any line hitherto and hence presented new problems of water- and coal-supply, the directors were soon claiming that they showed a saving of one-third over horse haulage. Other builders, too, supplied locomotives, and one of these, Timothy Hackworth, shares with Stephenson the credit for first setting his cylinders horizontally or at a slight angle to the track rather than vertically and so hammering directly down on to it. With this arrangement came the end of the complex trellis-work of overhead beams characteristic of the first generation of locomotives.

A Second Lull

SUCH developments did not go un-noticed elsewhere in the world, for in 1827 the 24-year-old Robert Stephenson visited America, saw the tramways being built there, and returned with at least one export order. This was from the Delaware & Hudson Canal company, which in 1828 or 1829 took delivery of the *America*—a typical Stephenson engine of the period, and the first locomotive to be seen in America.

The *America*, however, never entered active service and was instead succeeded by the *Stourbridge Lion*. This locomotive, built by a rival company, became the first engine actually to operate in the Americas. Stephenson was more fortunate with another commission, that for two locomotives built in 1828 to the design of French engineer Marc Seguin for a 38-mile railroad just opened between Lyons and St. Etienne: this was the first steam-operated track in Europe, though in the previous year a passenger-carrying horse line had been opened in Austria. A few more years were to witness orders coming in from Canada and elsewhere, thus justifying the historian G. M. Trevelyan's remark that railroads were England's gift to the world.

Yet in their homeland (which was now overcast by a post-war shortage of capital), railroads seemed to be suffering from another five-year lull, and the casual observer could see more activity in the direction of building the last of the horse tramways than in the laying-down of new locomotive lines. It was on paper that the forward-looking work was taking place now, with some half-dozen Parliamentary Acts for new railroads being passed every year, most of them making provision for the use of locomotives and for passenger traffic.

Such planning led to two lines which were opened in 1830. The humbler, but probably the earlier, was the Canterbury & Whitstable—all that survived from a plan by William James (who was obsessed by the security of the Channel) to by-pass the sea-lanes with a route through Kent. This survivor was only six miles long and typically made use of horses and of two long inclines, but it could boast of a half-mile tunnel—the longest yet built for railroad use. And though it owned only a single Stephenson engine (the *Invicta*), this was used, as no earlier line had used a locomotive, for the regular haulage of passengers.

The C & W was opened in May, 1830, and introduced the idea of railroads to a dubious south of England. But away in the north, some six months earlier, the public had witnessed the dramatic experiment which was to be the curtain-raiser to a new age.

Opening day on the Canterbury & Whitstable.
Unusual features are the single tracking and
Invicta's *tender design.*

Stephenson's Invicta, *sole engine of the Canterbury & Whitstable railroad. Note the square smoke-box (a later modification).*

The Liverpool & Manchester

THOUGH only some 30 miles long, the Liverpool & Manchester line was to remove the last obstacles before the realization of a railroad full-blooded and unqualified. Yet such was the temper of the age that even here there was no sudden leap towards the future but rather a cautious and half-accidental approach.

The story begins with the increasing dissatisfaction of the merchants of Manchester – and, even more, of Liverpool – at the high charges of the canal which linked them, and at the delays which meant that goods could take longer to travel overland than to arrive from America. For it is a comment on the road conditions then persisting that this canal had a virtual monopoly of that heavy transport between Liverpool and Manchester on which depended much of Britain's potential for manufacture, and for import and export to and from America. It was once more the energetic William James who overcame many false starts and opposition from vested interests, and who eventually saw a railroad approved with George Stephenson in charge.

At this time there was keen debate between the "cable" and the "locomotive" parties. Stephenson was no opponent of cableways, for he had used this system on his colliery line and, even five years after the L & M had proved itself, was to build a general-purpose railroad which used inclined planes. (At the same period, a passenger line was to be opened in London which depended on an endlessly moving cable.) But for the L & M Stephenson believed locomotives to be the right answer. So, when the tracks came to be built after surveys conducted under cover of darkness and along a route dictated as much by local interests as by technical considerations, a compromise was adopted. For most of the railroad's length gradients were restricted to the very modest figure of 1 in 1000, but two parts (in addition to the approach to the Liverpool terminus, which like other such city-center sections was to remain an anomaly for many years) were steepened to about 1 in 100.

Whether these could be handled by locomotives or not would have to be determined by experiment. Meanwhile the backers of the line decided to hold a locomotive competition, a rally rather than a race, open to all comers. Such were the Rainhill trials of 1829.

The Rainhill Trials

THE week-long event took place on a level section near the middle of the Liverpool & Manchester line, and created enormous public interest. The technical requirements were tough: for instance, weights were restricted, boilers had to be tested to three times their working pressures, and the atmosphere was not to be polluted. This last provision meant that coke had to be burned instead of coal, a practice which endured on British railroads for many years.

Although numerous engineers were attracted towards Rainhill, there survived on October 6 only five "runners"—and one of them was quite literally that, being a horse-worked contraption. One of the steam-powered contestants, too, proved an early failure, and another turned out to be technically overweight as well as somewhat unreliable.

Novelty—*the unsuccessful but odds-on favorite at the Rainhill trials of 1829.*

Sans Pareil, *Timothy Hackworth's entry for the Rainhill trials. It was disqualified on the grounds of weight.*

Robert Stephenson's Rocket *was a triumphal success. Note that here both driver and fireman could work from a conventional footplate position.*

This narrowed the field to Robert Stephenson's entry – the famous *Rocket*, whose most notable technical feature was a full multi-tube boiler – and a machine entered by two designers, one of whom was the Swedish John Ericsson. Despite its strange looks, its vertical boiler and its unconventional appendages such as a bellows to fan the fire, this *Novelty* became the public's favorite as it swept past the grandstand at speeds variously reported as between 20 and 40 mph. But Stephenson was not impressed. "That thing", he said, "has got no guts."

And so it proved, for as the ordeal neared its end the *Rocket* emerged a clear winner on the grounds of reliability alone. Furthermore, although hill-climbing formed no part of the Rainhill trials themselves, later experience showed that the *Rocket* was quite capable of handling the 1 in 100 gradients. The Stephensons could now concentrate on building-up a "stud" of eight *Rocket*-type engines, some of them incorporating the further improvement of a separate **smoke-box** (where the hot gases were gathered before being exhausted up the funnel) at the front end and others with a proper **tender** instead of a makeshift barrel in which to store the feed-water. These were ready for the grand opening of the Liverpool & Manchester railroad which was to take place just under a year later.

The First American Railroads

THE first full-sized locomotive to run in North America – the *Stourbridge Lion,* delivered in 1828 to the Delaware & Hudson canal company – had a very short life. For although American engineers had the advantage of benefiting from Britain's early mistakes and so of entering railroad technology in its second phase (with the inclined plane, however, enjoying a long life in America), they discovered problems of their own in adapting the locomotive to the lightly engineered tracks characteristic of a continent where distances were far longer in relation to population than in Europe.

The Delaware & Hudson's colliery line from Honesdale to Carbondale in Pennsylvania, with its 4 feet 3 inches gauge, was itself only some 20 miles in length. But it had a flimsy bridge and such sharp curves that on the maiden journey in August, 1829, its representative,

Horatio Allen, would trust nobody save himself on the footplate. Both Allen and his machine survived the journey, though Allen had never handled a locomotive before and was never to do so again; but the track, being of iron-plated timber rails, was so damaged by the experiment that the *Lion* was retired and horses took over instead, with the assistance of incline working. A similarly short active life was to be the fate of the first locomotive to work in the state of New York – the underpowered, Stephenson-type but locally-built *De Witt Clinton* which derailed on its maiden run in 1831.

In Baltimore, however, things were rather better planned. This city, isolated by hills from the main canal network of the eastern states,

was determined that it should become the terminus of an all-American railroad. This ambition was indeed so much bound up with national pride that when Charles Carroll, the last survivor of those who had signed the Declaration of Independence, came to inaugurate the substantial and double-tracked railroad more than fifty years later, he said that he regarded the two ceremonies as of almost equal importance.

The first locomotive of what was ambitiously named the Baltimore & Ohio railroad was hardly more than a toy. Built by Peter Cooper of New York in 1829, it weighed just over a ton and was aptly named *Tom Thumb*. As if to underline that it was a local product owing little to the English tradition, it embodied a vertical boiler – a feature which rarely appeared in European locomotives after the failure of the *Novelty*, but one which was to be characteristic of the first generation of American locomotives.

Early American railroads, however, kept a sharp eye on European developments. Little more than a year after the Rainhill trials and while the line was still mainly dependent on horses and mules, a similar competition was held on the B & O with the provision that all contestants should be home-built. The winner here was the *York*, a vertical-boilered engine built by Phineas Davis. Davis was by profession a watchmaker, but he had enlarged the scale of his engineering skills so successfully that the last of the eighteen machines of his *York* class (called "grasshoppers" since they preserved an old-fashioned and elaborate overhead motion) saw service until almost the end of the century and similar locomotives were soon being exported to Europe.

Local public operations, including the carriage of passengers, began on the B & O early in 1830. In the following year another line, the Mohawk & Hudson, started work with a Stephenson locomotive. By 1835 the Baltimore railroad had been extended to a length of nearly 80 miles, and it could also boast a brick-built terminal station completed in its year of foundation. Whether Baltimore, Canterbury or Manchester should receive the title of the world's first custom-built station is perhaps an open question, a matter of months; but, certainly 1830 was a landmark year for the railroads of two hemispheres.

Opposite *The* Stourbridge Lion, *purchased in England for the Delaware & Hudson Company, introduced practical steam locomotion to America in 1828.*

Below. *A slightly-enlarged replica of the vertical-boilered* Tom Thumb. *For all its low power, this was America's first home-built locomotive.*

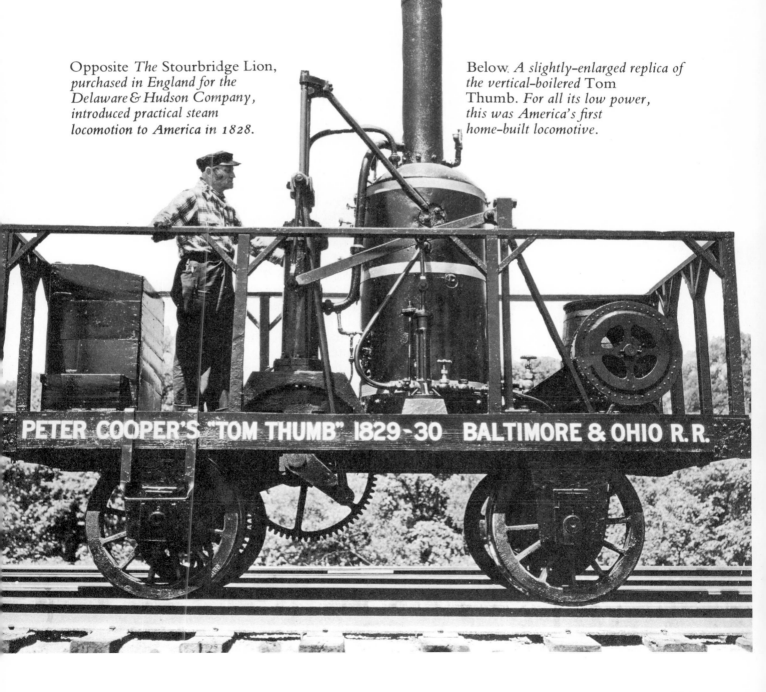

PETER COOPER'S "TOM THUMB" 1829-30 BALTIMORE & OHIO R.R.

Opening Day

SEPTEMBER 15, 1830 is perhaps the most famous date of all British transport history. At Manchester, at Liverpool, along the tracks between them and in the painted open wagons and stagecoach-like carriages a crowd of tens, if not hundreds, of thousands awaited the fanfares and booming cannon which sent the inaugural trains on their way. For this was the world's first line to fulfill all the conditions of a modern railroad—a stout reserved track, partial public control plus full public availability and accountability, and the regular and scheduled haulage of passengers as well as of freight behind steam locomotives in stock which (in contrast to canal and some tramway practice) was owned by the railroad company itself.

Among the faceless and anonymous that day there were many whose names are still familiar. There was George Stephenson himself, of course, top-hatted on the footplate, now a national hero and with a son soon to become just as famous. There was an eleven-year-old boy named Edward Watkin, who was to dominate the later railroad age and live

to be its last tycoon. There was Mr Huskisson, fated to die a few hours later—an event immortalized in Thomas Baker's poem since it ". . . not only caused delay/But damped the joy that erst had crown'd the day." There was the Duke of Wellington—an opponent of railroads, which he thought would only make protest easier for the angry working classes of the period, but included on this occasion as guest of honor and seated in a coronet-adorned state coach. And in contrast there was the delicious and observant actress Fanny Kemble, who confessed herself "horribly in love" with Stephenson, who regarded a locomotive as something to be affectionately patted like a horse, but who, as a 21-year-old veteran of an earlier visit, noted how swiftly George Stephenson's work was already blending into the English landscape.

The railroad structures built at this time, and for the most part still in service today, were themselves of a massiveness which the world had not witnessed in a transport context since the age of the Caesars. There was the Olive Mount cutting, for instance—an impressive work, if not quite the "awful chasm" of contemporary descriptions. There were bridges

Scenes on the Liverpool & Manchester railroad.

Opposite *Newton-le-Willows*.

Below *Entrance to Manchester across Water Street.*

Bottom *Stephenson's skew bridge near Rainhill.*

and viaducts rising up to 70 feet above the valleys: such works, with their piers of brick or masonry climbing to segmental arches, were to set their stamp not only on all Britain but on far lands where the British railroad-builders worked. Just as notable, if less regarded by the public, was Stephenson's marsh crossing, which was achieved by the sinking of rafts of brushwood until a firm bed could be established. And in Manchester there was a fine custom-built station.

The Liverpool & Manchester Railway was an immediate commercial success. But it held a surprise for its sponsors in that the

receipts for passenger traffic were soon exceeding those from freight. Indeed, freight handling fell in arrears as every engine was impressed for the unexpected commuter traffic. Though without the disastrous consequences foreseen by Wellington, men were no longer bound to their parish or their block of a few streets; and Dr Arnold, the great headmaster of Rugby school who welcomed railroads as marking the end of feudal England, was to prove wiser than those fellow-educators who were soon to ban railroads from approaching Eton on the grounds that the place would become inundated by French governesses.

Several classes of passenger, as well as freight and livestock, carried by the Liverpool and Manchester Railway.

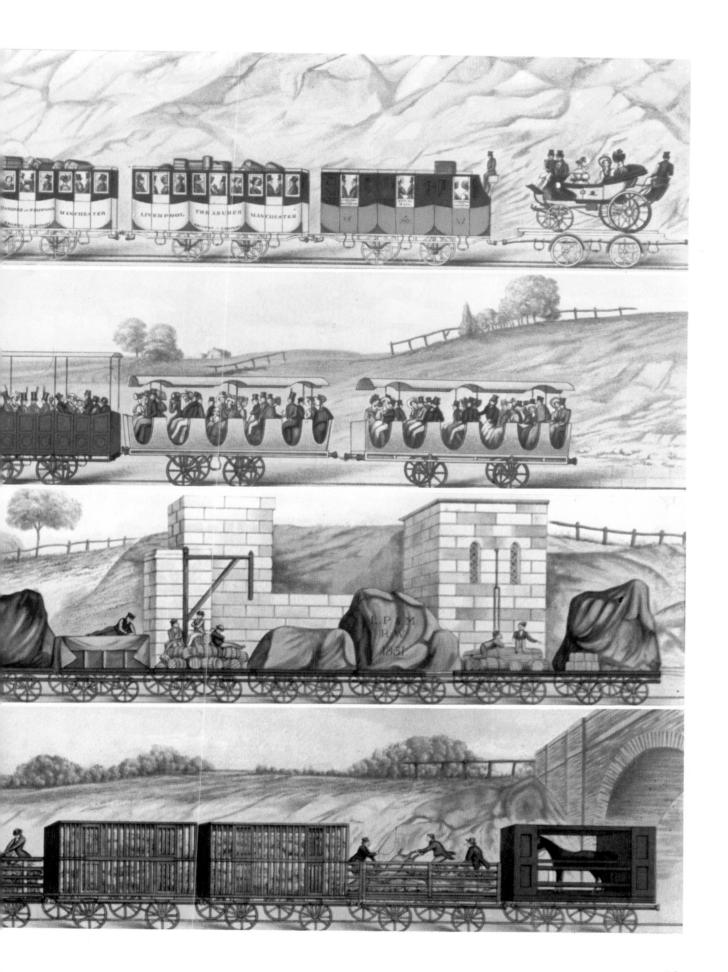

EFFECTS OF THE RAILROAD ON THE BRUTE CREATION

Transition

THE brief reign of William IV from 1830 to 1837 witnessed no great railroad landmarks in Britain, and at first sight seems to form another period of stock-taking before the excitements of the railroad explosion of the Victorian era. But in fact this was an age of progress on many fronts.

A number of new lines were constructed, for instance, and though mostly short, these were stoutly engineered. (Typical of them was London's own first railroad: supported throughout on a brick viaduct, this was conceived as part of a "grand processional boulevard" extending from the capital through Greenwich to the coast and was opened with musical honors supplied by bandsmen dressed as Beefeaters). Simultaneously many of the old horse-tramways were rebuilt to accommodate powered traction, so that this period saw the end draw in sight for a medium which had, in its time, served the country well. The canals which had previously been the ally of land transport were also entering into a period of contraction. In 1832, for example, they carried over 10,000 tons of coal to London, but well before the end of the decade the figure had fallen to virtually zero.

To cope with the increasing trade of the dozen or more railroads now using locomotives, designers such as Edward Bury (whose characteristic haycock-shaped firebox became as familiar in America as in Britain) built engines with weights closer to 20 tons than the 5 or 10 tons common in the 1820s, and both passenger and freight rolling stock took their first faltering steps away from being merely adaptations of road carriages. Despite stout opposition from the landed gentry and their gamekeepers, from canal and stage-coach interests, and not least from physicians who believed that any travel above 10 mph was dangerous and that tunnels meant certain death, the public too was coming to accept the concept of the railroad with its new standards

London & Greenwich Railway Company.

THIS TICKET WILL ADMIT

William Beloe, Esquire

from 19. January 1837 to 19. April 1837.

NOT TRANSFERABLE.

Nº 60 Third Class

I. Y. Akerman, Sec.ᵞ

Opposite *A comment of 1831 – rather gentler than most – on the way the railroads might put an older means of transport out of business.*

Left *The line running from south of London Bridge to Deptford (and later Greenwich) was not only London's first: it claimed to be the first anywhere to offer "season" or commuter rates.*

Below *A German artist's impression of London's first railroad. Flag signals controlled operations.*

of speed and mobility. The metaphorical signal-lights (for it was to be some years before any railroad could show a device closer to a *real* signal than a "policeman" holding a flag) had for long been set at caution: now they exhibited a clear and unambiguous green.

But nowhere in Britain as yet could one find a line more than a couple of dozen miles in length, for the true trunk railroad raised new legal as well as technical problems in an already-congested land. Not surprisingly, then, it was some years in the planning. But, fittingly enough, it was ready for its opening at the dawn of Queen Victoria's reign.

Above *Satire on Britain's first railroad boom after 1836, which was in fact far better-founded than the mania which followed nearly a decade later.*

Opposite top *One of Scotland's earliest railroads was the Glasgow & Garnkirk. This illustration captures the opening-day splendors.*

Opposite bottom *A scene on the London & Grenwich railroad, showing the typical viaduct construction used throughout by its engineer, George Landmann.*

The labor force assembled by Thomas Brassey to build the Paris–Rouen line are shown at their celebratory dinner.

The First Trunk Line

FROM London to the manufacturing city of Birmingham was more than 110 miles, even by a route far more direct than William James' projected way via Stratford. Over those miles Robert Stephenson plodded on foot or horseback some 15 times as he surveyed and supervised the great arterial railroad which was eventually to connect the two cities. In 1823 he was still only 30 years old, but there had been few protests when a man so young was put in charge of so huge and unprecedented a work.

Perhaps the greatest challenge to him was less technical than human. Even the comparatively modest Stockton & Darlington and Liverpool & Manchester lines had posed to Robert's father entirely new problems of management, but the building of the London & Birmingham was a work on at least four times this scale and at its peak employed some 20,000 men. According to contemporary writers, indeed, it could be compared in magnitude only to the Pyramids or to the Great Wall of China. And all this had to be undertaken with only the addition of gunpowder to give more mechanical aid than was known to the Egyptians, for though at one stage Stephenson employed steam-powered drainage pumps his primitive earth-drills, cranes, pile-drivers and temporary tracks were all worked by animal power or human muscles. Those muscles were furnished by gangs which were to transform the face of Britain throughout the nineteenth century, but which made their greatest impact before 1850. A nucleus of experienced labor bearing the name of "navigators" or **navvies** was provided by men who had learnt their skills in forming cuttings, embankments and tunnels on the last of the canals, but the scale of their operations in the railroad age was to be considerably greater than before. And so Stephenson set up the first of those manpower structures which were to become common in British railroad construction, structures of contractors and subcontractors extending down to the self-employed ganger who, with half a dozen mates, toted his labor from site to site with spade in hand and wheelbarrow on back. At first the unskilled force was largely recruited locally. Later, dispossessed peasants from the Scottish Highlands joined the gangs: and in the 1840s the Irish potato famine was to add its own quota of hungry men.

Not surprisingly these groups were unpopular with each other, and most certainly they were unpopular with the local residents who went in terror of their wild ways. Nor did the conditions of their life help, for the navvies were housed in crude and overcrowded huts, paid well but at such long intervals that they were regularly in debt or overdrawn at the company "truck" shops, fed well (on two pounds of beef a day) but monotonously, and offered no recreation save drink. Indeed, it was said that for every mile of line built in Britain £100 was spent on liquor.

For this reason alone, fights and needless accidents became a way of life. But these men shifted their 100 foot-tons of spoil each day, and there emerged those engineering works which are still typical of some 10,000 miles of British railroad track. These viaducts and tunnel-portals are for the most part built in a proud, no-nonsense, north-country style which forms a link between the elegance of the Georgian age and the floridity of late Victoriana, and they are well exemplified on the London & Birmingham railroad.

Early gangs of navvies building the Hampstead Road bridge on the London & Birmingham railroad.

Above *An early German main line ran from Berlin to Potsdam. Note the turntable, a feature of many original station arrangements.*

Below Der Alder, *an example of Robert Stephenson's "Patentee" locomotives, which ran on the first all-German line from Nuremberg to Fürth, in 1835.*

Opposite top *Scenes on the first French line, opened between Lyons and St Etienne in 1829.*

Opposite bottom *Although built by the agnostic Englishman Joseph Locke, the first French trunk route—from Paris to Le Havre—was inaugurated with full pontifical honors.*

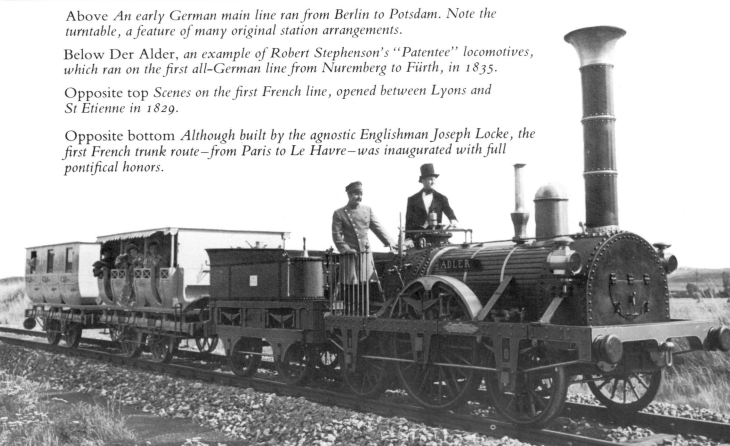

Man against Nature

IN the course of building the London & Birmingham – the "Brummagen line" – Robert Stephenson had to cross two watersheds and two valleys between his temporary, cable-worked London terminus and his finely built railhead at Curzon Street, Birmingham. The valleys presented few problems, though they necessitated constructing the most substantial metal bridges yet built for a railroad. But the hills called for two heroic cuttings – one through the chalk of the Chilterns, the other through Northamptonshire ironstone – and also, in the latter area, the most ambitious tunnel which railroad engineers had yet attempted. This, twin-tracked and $1\frac{1}{4}$ miles long, was at Kilsby near Rugby.

Here Stephenson was unlucky in that, despite his careful surveys and test-bores, he hit a buried spring. After his contractor had died of the shock, Robert took over in person to organize a work which cost five times as much per foot as the rest of the line, progressed correspondingly slowly, and took 26 lives. But when the Kilsby tunnel – and, with it, the entire line – was opened in 1838, it represented the first of those sagas of endurance and improvization which were to characterize railroad construction throughout the world.

The Two Engineerings

THERE was nothing revolutionary about the trackwork of the "Brummagen": its rails were short and of I section, and though they were usually mounted on the timber sleepers whose merits had now been proved in America, Stephenson was conservative enough to use stone blocks on some stretches. Nor did the layout of the line as a whole deviate from the principles which his father had adopted in Lancashire. But the very fact that these principles were displayed on no mere local railroad but on one which swept across more than 100 miles to enter the nation's capital highlights those features of railway building which were to be characteristic of the British school.

In this school the works of earth and brick, masonry and metal, were substantial, and due attention was paid to such details as drainage. Curves were of generous radius (commonly a mile), and as the age progressed and technical knowledge increased the problems of leading a line gently into a bend and of **canting** or **super-elevating** the outer rail were worked out in the interests of safe and steady riding. Above all, gradients were so rigidly restricted that on the L & B Stephenson rarely exceeded 1 in 300.

This proved to be a very expensive way to

build a railroad, and there were soon more or less well-informed critics to protest at such high standards. But over the years the substructures laid down by Stephenson and his colleagues were to serve Britain magnificently. They may have appeared over-ambitious or over-cautious in an era of light and comparatively slow trains, but the L & B exists today as part of Britain's arterial rail system with its barely strengthened viaducts carrying a dense traffic of electrified freight and passenger trains of some five times Stephensonian weight at perhaps three times Stephensonian speeds.

Civil engineering, then, entered the railroad age in an almost over-perfected form. By contrast, British locomotive design was still in an advanced infancy characterized by high chimneys and open footplates. The most popular style of engine in the mid-1830s was Robert Stephenson's own *Patentee* type–a six-wheeler, with the cylinders set rather inaccessibly inside the frame, incorporating an innovation in the form of a steam-operated brake.

Many hundreds of these *Patentees* were built, but they proved so popular on the short prototype lines which were now springing up in one European country after another that Stephenson had to go to his rival Edward Bury for motive power for the L & B itself. And this power came in the form of the little four-wheelers, displaying Bury's characteristic tall firebox, which had to be marshaled together two, three, four or even five times over to haul their 100-ton trains up Stephenson's gentle gradients.

A working shaft of the Kilsby tunnel.

*The crossing of Chat Moss on the Liverpool &
Manchester railroad.*

A Momentous Year

THE year 1836, which had seen the start
of building on the London & Birmingham line, was a momentous one for Britain's
railroads as a whole. In or around that year
some half-dozen other major schemes were
initiated, all of which were to result in lines
completed about 1840. For example, there
were soon three railroads crossing the main-
land from coast to coast, one linking Glasgow
and Edinburgh, another being the rather
isolated and backward-looking Newcastle &
Carlisle, and the third forming a more daring
crossing of England's spine, the Pennine chain.
This last, the Leeds & Manchester railroad
which involved a substantial tunnel through
rock, was one of a whole group which the
Stephensons built in the Midlands and as far
north as York during this era.

Yet the first and the most important of this
northern group of lines was that which,
though only some 80 miles long, bore the
impressive title of the Grand Junction railroad.
The name is also a clue to its function, for,
with Manchester and Liverpool linked by
rail and plans approved for the London &
Birmingham line to be constructed with the
same general characteristics, it was an obvious
move to join the two systems by way of a
railroad running north from Birmingham to
a convenient point on the L & M. Work on
the Grand Junction was indeed both begun and
completed before that on the L & B itself, so
that well before 1840 England had a network
linking its four most important cities. Men and
freight could now travel nearly 200 miles from
London to Manchester and Liverpool, though
for the passengers a change of stations in
Birmingham was necessary at first.

The engineer of the Grand Junction was a one-time colleague of the Stephensons, Joseph Locke, who had now set up on his own. Even before the GJ was complete, Locke was to be engaged on another major project in the south, and there it became clear that his concepts differed from those of the Stephensons: he had a marked dislike of tunnels, for example, and was prepared to deflect his route in order to avoid them. He was also ready to accept rather sharper gradients than his rivals, though 1 in 175 was hardly steep. Between Birmingham and the mid-point of the L & M, however, the country was so level that Locke's line was able to run for mile after mile with hardly a deviation from a crow's-flight course, and to cost only about one-third of the rate per mile of the "Brummagen" line.

The GJ is noteworthy for three reasons other than its confident engineering. One is that it established Crewe, hitherto a "green fields" site, as a major example of those well-planned artificial towns which were to be characteristic of the British railroad age. Another is that Locke devised a form of rolled rail which was throughout mounted via chairs on timber sleepers. This rail originally took a simple dumb-bell form, the idea being that when one face became worn down it could be turned over so that the other edge was exposed. Practice did not obey theory, however, and so the cross-section was modified to that of an inverted figure 8 with the larger bulge set uppermost. This **bull-head rail** then proved the longest-lasting type which had as yet been employed. Although it was to be produced in ever-heavier forms and ever-greater lengths over the decades, its basic form so long outlived the age of wrought iron that it remained the norm on Britain's railroads for a full century.

Finally, Locke turned away from Stephenson's system of contractors and sub-contractors, some of whom had proved so unreliable and under-funded that a third of even the L & B's main suppliers went bankrupt. For most of the work on the GJ, Locke relied instead on a single builder, Thomas Brassey, a fine engineer in his own right and a man of the highest integrity. Controlling at one period a labor force of over 100,000 and a budget equal to that of a small nation, Brassey was to go on to lay nearly 2000 miles of track in Britain alone, while the overseas activities which began with his building of a historic route from Paris to Normandy were later to extend from the Grand Trunk railroad in Canada to a military line which was to recoup the effects of imbecile generalship in the Crimean war.

Opposite *J. C. Bourne's famous illustration shows the way in which barrows of spoil were perilously hauled up to form such embankments as this on the Birmingham line.*

Below *A signaling device which has survived unchanged after 130 years is the explosive detonator. Here, a fogman sensibly flees from the approaching uproar.*

Below *The long and deep cutting through the Northamptonshire rock at Blisworth—typical of early British railroad engineering.*

Bottom *The "horizontal-arched" portal of Primrose Hill tunnel, the most southerly on the London & Birmingham line.*

A view on the North Midland line, showing alternative transport of the 1840s—packhorse and canal-boat.

Early Stations

THROUGHOUT the world the coming of the railroad age involved not only engineering achievements but a host of peripheral activities, and as the pioneer nation Britain had had to take the first steps with many of these. Not the least of innovations, for instance, was that of the passenger station.

This was not the only type of architectural structure needed by the new transport medium. Freight depots too were required, though for these the warehouses of the canal age provided some precedents, and there was a host of specialized buildings ranging from the first, lighthouse-like signal boxes to engine sheds. Of these latter, the classic precedent is the Roundhouse at the top of the bank leading up from Euston to Camden Town: this was built in 1837, and though a more economical and polygonal form of stable was introduced on the Croydon railroad in the next year, the roundhouse structure was to be so distinctive of these early years that in America the term became almost a synonym for an engine shed.

One slightly later line in the Midlands was the Birmingham & Derby, whose badge is shown here.

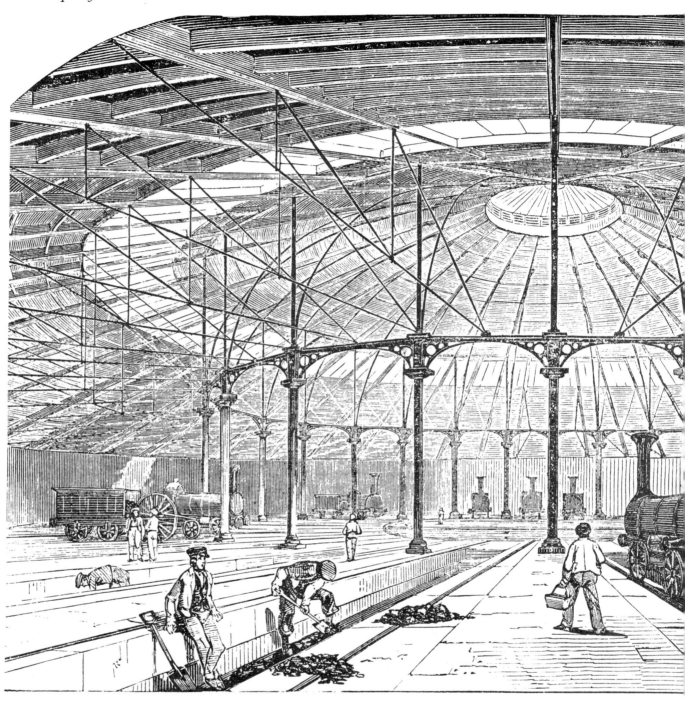

Interior of the Roundhouse, 1847. This entirely circular engine shed formed part of the Camden Town depot of the North Western railroad.

Yet it was through the station that the young railroads met their most mistrustful customers. The problem of making them feel at ease had two facets, and of these the easier to dispose of was the design of the way station serving a community of up to some 10,000 inhabitants. It is true that neither the inn-yards of the stage-coach era (which handled at most a few dozen passengers at a time) nor the wharf where the occasional passenger might join a canal-boat provided a precedent here, nor could the pioneer lines themselves show much in the way of intermediate stations. Yet with the coming of the comparatively obscure Newcastle & Carlisle railroad in the late 1830s there sprang up—almost as if from the soil, almost as closely attuned to it as a parish church, and despite all researches apparently anonymously—a type of station building which was to prove a model for the whole of Britain. It was to be broadly copied overseas too, though in America timber was a commoner structural material

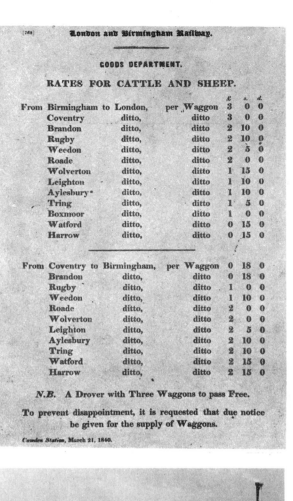

[765]

London and Birmingham Railway.

GOODS DEPARTMENT.

RATES FOR CATTLE AND SHEEP.

			£	s.	d.
From Birmingham to London,	per Waggon		3	0	0
Coventry	ditto,	ditto	3	0	0
Brandon	ditto,	ditto	2	10	0
Rugby	ditto,	ditto	2	10	0
Weedon	ditto,	ditto	2	5	0
Roade	ditto,	ditto	2	0	0
Wolverton	ditto,	ditto	1	15	0
Leighton	ditto,	ditto	1	10	0
Aylesbury	ditto,	ditto	1	10	0
Tring	ditto,	ditto	1	5	0
Boxmoor	ditto,	ditto	1	0	0
Watford	ditto,	ditto	0	15	0
Harrow	ditto,	ditto	0	15	0
From Coventry to Birmingham,	per Waggon		0	18	0
Brandon	ditto,	ditto	0	18	0
Rugby	ditto,	ditto	1	0	0
Weedon	ditto,	ditto	1	10	0
Roade	ditto,	ditto	2	0	0
Wolverton	ditto,	ditto	2	0	0
Leighton	ditto,	ditto	2	5	0
Aylesbury	ditto,	ditto	2	10	0
Tring	ditto,	ditto	2	10	0
Watford	ditto,	ditto	2	15	0
Harrow	ditto,	ditto	2	15	0

N.B. A Drover with Three Waggons to pass Free.

To prevent disappointment, it is requested that due notice be given for the supply of Waggons.

Camden Station, March 21, 1840.

A panorama of the Camden yards showing early pointwork and the chimneys of the stationary engine which worked the cable of the incline.

than stone or brick and the carriage-level platform was to remain a British luxury.

Perhaps the basic plan of such small stations was to an extent inevitable, considering the need for staff accommodation, waiting-rooms and **booking office**—this latter term deriving from the early practice of logging passengers on a manifest rather than simply selling tickets to them, a stage of clumsiness from which the world's airlines are only now emerging. But they also provided the opportunity for the adoption of characteristic architectural styles, where every cast-iron capital or carpentered valence offered a chance to display individual taste. Overall, two idioms became especially favored in Britain: a variant on Tudor or Jacobean architecture was more favored in rural sites, while small urban stations often turned to that elegant, villa-like mode which is called Italianate but which was, in fact, largely the invention of the railroad architects of the early 1840s.

Termini

MORE considerable were the problems inherent in the design of the big-city stations which stood in relation to the minor ones as did a cathedral to a parish church.

These might be either through-stations (in which case an enlargement of the type mentioned above provided a basis) or true, dead-end termini. The latter were to become common in Europe: they had the disadvantage that through trains had to reverse, but the advantage that the station building could be brought into the heart of the city without the expense of providing two channels of land for access tracks. By contrast, Britain was by 1840 already so urbanized that even in major cities the principal station tended to be some distance from the center and served by through lines. The situation was further complicated by a multiplication of companies which might, or might not, be prepared to share facilities. But even in Britain there was a need for the great headquarters-station, and so here too pioneers had to find an appropriate plan.

This proved a surprisingly difficult matter. Indeed, the problem of providing suitable metropolitan railheads for such lines as the

Top and above *Two views of a model of the original Euston station, London's first rail gateway to the north. The humble train sheds contrast with the grandeur of Philip Hardwick's great Doric arch and flanking pavilions.*

Opposite top *The interior of the train shed at Euston.*

Opposite bottom *The entrance to the engine sheds at the top of the Camden incline.*

BIRMINGHAM RAILWAY STATION.

Great Western Railway was for some reason postponed for some years after 1840. Part of the trouble was that in the early days of the railroads waiting passengers were not sure how the new beasts should be regarded. At first the public treated locomotives with an exaggerated respect, but after a year or so they had become so much a part of the scene that travelers felt they were simply changing coaches in an inn-yard and hence milled around the tracks, with the inevitable consequences. This led the companies to keep their passengers under a strict surveillance which resembles airport practice today, and which was paralleled by the dangerous practice of locking them into their compartments *en route*.

Another failing of the first termini was that it was considered that one arrival and one departure platform should serve all needs: between them there might be a number of "stabling" tracks, but as these were connected by turntables more often than by points train-marshaling was a tedious operation. It was not until well into the 1840s that the plan of having a concourse or head platform from

which a number of fingers extended was generally adopted, and another improvement—the great overall roof of glass and curved iron ribs—did not appear much before 1850.

Meanwhile, something had to be done to inform the public of London and a few other major cities of the solidity of the companies which would carry them across Britain; for whereas in rural sites the problem had been to create a note of friendly familiarity, one purpose of the civic station was to impress potential investors. Birmingham could from the start show a building as classically impressive as a bank, and soon Bristol was to have its counterpart in the rival Gothic mode. What then was to be the reply of the world's greatest city? Even if the accommodation for trains and travelers in London's termini was still in an experimental stage, some gesture of grandeur had to be made, and so a compromise solution was reached. This was to invest the approaches to termini with grand porticos or colonnades, the supreme example being the archway which stood before Euston until its recent vandalization.

No.95

OPENING
OF THE
AYLESBURY RAILWAY.

Dinner Ticket,
WHITE HART INN,
Monday, June 10th, 1839.

10s.   *Dinner on Table at 4 o'Clock.*

Opposite *The fine façade of Curzon Street station, Birmingham—the still-standing terminus of Robert Stephenson's great trunk line.*

Left *The brief spur to Aylesbury, which left the main London & Birmingham railroad at Cheddington in the Chilterns, was probably the first of all Britain's rural branch lines.*

Below *Berkhamsted, in the Chiltern country, is one of the many sites where the rail and canal routes from London to Birmingham run almost shoulder-to-shoulder.*

Model of Marc Seguin's first locomotive for the Lyon & St Etienne railroad (1829), scenes of which appear on page 33.

An artist's impression of Robert Stephenson's Northumbrian, *the first locomotive to be built with an integral firebox.*

A locomotive with Edward Bury's distinctive boiler at Camden freight station in 1840.

Into America

ALMOST from the start, the North American railroad system had branched off in a direction so different from the British one that there were contrasts even in terminology.

That this was so was largely due to the differences between an already developed, populous and industrialized land and a young nation whose main assets were space and faith. On the eastern seaboard the task was to get the rails down as quickly and as cheaply as possible, and there were rarely either the needs or the facilities for sophisticated surveys and massive engineering works. While Britain was building its fine masonry viaducts, America was spanning gorges on crazy-looking timber trestles: while Britain was developing substantial iron rails, America was using timber tracks whose facings had an alarming habit of "shake-heading" up through the floors of carriages: while Britain was fencing its lines to an ultra-safe standard, America was permitting the main streets of new towns to shape themselves along unprotected railroads: and while Britain remained worried by a few miles of 1 in 100 gradients, America accepted such steepness for leagues on end.

With methods so simplified, progress was swift, so that by 1836 – the year when Canada's first metals were laid – North America could show some 1000 route-miles of line, over twice as much as Britain and half of the world's total. In one respect, too, America could already claim superiority – the matter of **loading gauge** or the clearance allowed to rolling-stock both laterally by the nearness of platform edges and the like and vertically by the height of bridges and tunnels. With major engineering works so rare by European (and, especially, by British) standards, and with a general ambience of spaciousness, America could increase clearances by as much as 50 per cent above English norms, with benefits which the future was to show.

Such contrasts in trackwork were reflected in mechanical engineering too, for if only to cope with the steep gradients of American lines more powerful locomotives were called for. (These were usually built by independent concerns such as the Baldwin company rather than by the railroads themselves as had become the practice in Britain.) The engines of the period, normally weighing under 15 tons, were still lightweight by later standards. But that American designs soon acquired a reputation for power is shown by the fact that, as early as 1840, a British company ordered Philadelphia-built locomotives to work its more difficult routes. A few years later freight engines could be seen in America with the hitherto unknown feature of eight coupled driving wheels, though the most popular passenger type was undoubtedly the 4–4–0.

On their home ground, American locomotives early acquired those accessories which were so characteristic at first sight. The prevalence of unfenced tracks, for instance, led to the use of warning bells, headlamps and "chime" whistles – the last of these being introduced, fittingly enough, by the George Whistler who was not only a surveyor for the Baltimore & Ohio company but father of the famous artist and husband of "Whistler's Mother". Just as conspicuous were the huge spark-arresting funnels of the wood-burners, the roomy enclosed cabs, the sand-boxes which helped to defeat swarms of locusts as well as icy rails, and not least the cowcatcher patented by Isaac Dripps (who, as an apprentice, had been successful in putting a Stephenson locomotive together when it arrived at Philadelphia as a kit without instructions for assembly) which meant that after a collision a railroad company usually had to pay for a new steer rather than a new engine.

More important than all these, however, was the fact that the tight radii of American lines called for an easing of trains round curves by use of a device which had been invented but forgotten in Britain, the pivoted pony-truck or bogie whose rediscovery is attributed to J. B. Jervis (the designer of the *De Witt Clinton*) and the versatile Horatio Allen. The derailments of locomotives such as the *John Bull* which lacked this aid was indeed an early incentive towards an independent school of American design, and the bogie soon appeared on rolling stock too.

Two Traditions

MANY of these characteristics appeared on the second important public line to operate in America. As has been noted, the Baltimore & Ohio began like the Stockton & Darlington with a considerable use of horse haulage for its public services; but the South Carolina railroad, opened from Charleston on the Christmas day of 1830, was more a counter-

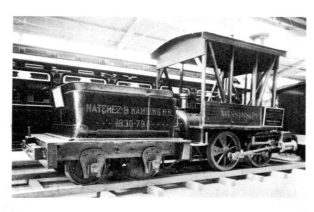

Top *An early American locomotive,* Sandusky, *of 1831, built by Rogers, Ketchum & Grosvenor.*

Middle *The* Mississippi, *1834, probably built by H. R. Dunham & Company was originally used on a pioneering railroad operation east out of Natchez.*

Bottom *The* Mazeppa, *built in 1837, worked on the Baltimore & Ohio railroad. Locomotives of this type were known as "crabs" because they appeared to run backwards.*

part of the Liverpool & Manchester in that after brief experiments with animal and even sail traction, it became fully committed to steam. That this was so was largely due to the faith of Horatio Allen again, for he believed that although in 1830 the arguments for equine and mechanical haulage almost balanced each other out, the breed of locomotives was a great deal more likely to improve than that of horses.

As perhaps the greatest pioneer of American railroads Allen had need of such faith, for the road's first locomotive, the *Best Friend of Charleston,* shortly blew itself up. In this fate it resembled its similarly vertical-boilered British contemporary the *Novelty,* though the *Best Friend's* end was speeded by the action of a fireman who strapped down the safety-valve to gain a little more power. It was succeeded by the *South Carolina,* another unconventional locomotive (it had two boilers arranged symmetrically about a central cab on what was later to be called the Fairlie pattern) which also caused some troubles. But the line itself prospered and after three years had been extended to 136 miles, so becoming by far the world's longest at the period. It was built to the gauge of 5 feet which was widely copied throughout the southern states.

It is worth noting that these British and American patterns, which had diverged even before 1835, were to provide prototypes for most of the world's railroads: only Germany was to devise a style characteristically its own. In the relatively prosperous and populous countries of Western Europe the Stephensonian model was followed, with its finely-engineered roads, its heavy investment in fixed equipment and its locomotives designed for stability and speed rather than power. But even in Britain itself standards were to be relaxed as branches proliferated later in the century; and deeper in Europe, in Asia, and in pioneer lands everywhere the American style was more usually followed. For instance, the first penetration of the Alps was made in Austria after an engineer from that country had inspected an extension of the Baltimore & Ohio line in 1842 and had been impressed by its handling of gradients of nearly 1 in 50 in the Alleghenies—the kind of country which, Robert Stephenson was still claiming, could be conquered only by cable working.

In North America, then, comparatively powerful locomotives with their weight distributed over several axles largely overcame the handicap of roughly laid, poorly finished and cheap single tracks. Increased fuel costs could be offset against the saving of interest on heavy fixed installations, and there was always the promise of financing later improvements out of revenue. "No one worries much about choosing the shortest route . . . or about gradients, and they scorn such things as gates at level-crossings . . . the line goes up hill-sides [and] scrambles down into valleys . . . It is not costly . . . but the trains have a habit of running off the rails," wrote Jules Verne more than thirty years later; and the novelist was not greatly exaggerating even then.

Southern England

THE homeland of railroads had been the north of England, and their first purpose was to transport freight. After the success of the L & M as a passenger-carrier, though, it became clear that there was a great potential market among those needing to make journeys for business or pleasure. So, although the first trunk railroad south from London was extended to the commercial port of Shoreham, its chief purpose was to improve communications between the capital and the favorite pleasure-ground for Londoners of all classes—the little fishing-village of Brighthelmstone which the Prince Regent and the stage-coach age had transformed into Brighton-on-Sea.

The London end of this line was already in existence, inasmuch as it branched off the Greenwich railroad. Furthermore, a spur from this had reached Croydon, creating a suburban traffic so dense (for there was by 1838 a rush-hour train every five minutes) that the world's first true signal-box had been erected at the junction. But for over 40 miles south from Croydon a trunk route was demanded, one which had to burrow through not only two ranges of chalk downs but a central hump of clay—and also had to cross a wide valley, this last being achieved by way of a most elegant viaduct.

The route of the Brighton line had been finally chosen from six competitors after the intervention of the government. In 1836 Parliament realized, too, that railroads were so important to the nation that a uniform gauge should be used. But that the intervention was a half-hearted one is shown by the story of London's linkage with the west.

One great system here has already been referred to, for it was the second major enterprise of Locke and Brassey, a line which linked London to Southampton and (less directly) to Portsmouth. This route showed Locke's dislike of tunneling, for the downlands were crossed mainly by means of deep cuttings which represented the displacement of over three million cubic yards of chalk. But basically the London and South Western was a conventional, if very finely engineered, railway of this pioneering period.

Much less conventional was its neighbor and future competitor, which from the start took the noble title of the Great Western Railway.

Brunel and the Great Western

EVER since the success of the Liverpool & Manchester line, the merchants of the old-established port of Bristol had been agitating for their own railroad. As the connection of Liverpool through to London drew in sight this pressure naturally increased. And in 1835 a chief engineer was appointed to the proposed Bristol railroad, Isambard Kingdom Brunel.

At that time, Brunel was only 29 years old, younger even than Robert Stephenson. Almost alone among the handful of pioneers who carved out the form of Britain's and thence the world's railroads, he had no connection with the Stephensons and their mine-based school; indeed, he had no particular railroad knowledge and little engineering experience of any kind. His background was that of a farming family from Normandy, and most of his training had consisted of assisting his father, Mark, on such projects as the first tunnel below the Thames. Yet somehow the merchants of Bristol had laid their hands on a unique genius, a man whose energy and talents seemed to strain the bounds of even those years around 1840 when in Britain nothing seemed impossible.

Brunel began by re-thinking the whole idea of a railroad. By now, 4 feet 8½ inches was regarded as the **standard gauge**: it was adopted on almost all Britain's major lines (though one system, reaching north-eastward from London, was to experiment briefly with a slightly wider spacing); it was beginning to penetrate Europe, and it was accepted too in the north-eastern states of America—though as the railroads there spread across the nation a wide variety of gauges from 2 feet to 6 feet

and above were employed locally. But Brunel insisted that a gauge of no less than 7 feet was essential if his vision of smooth, high-speed riding was to become a reality.

Whether it would have been better for the world's railroads had they adopted from the start a gauge broader than that used in Stephenson's collieries is a question which must here remain unresolved. What is certain is that Brunel came too late to revolutionize the lines of Britain, that his "balk" tracks proved over-rigid and led to washouts and derailments, and that in any case he failed to take full advantage of his costly broad way to the west. GWR rolling-stock, for example, was not much more spacious than was common at the time, and speeds were low—if only because there was little money left for motive power. Brunel was, in fact, not greatly interested in steam technology, and it was left to his young colleague Daniel Gooch to patch up the company's little engines—of which only one proved truly reliable. Nearly another decade was to pass before the GWR sorted out its traction troubles and began to set up such world speed records as 57 mph in regular service and a breathtaking 67 mph on one special run in 1848.

Early scenes on the Great Western.

Above *The interior of the freight shed at Bristol.*

Opposite top *The engine-shed at Swindon.*

Opposite bottom *The portal of Brunel's Box tunnel near Bath, built far higher than was necessary so as to provide an advertisement for the line visible from the nearby road.*

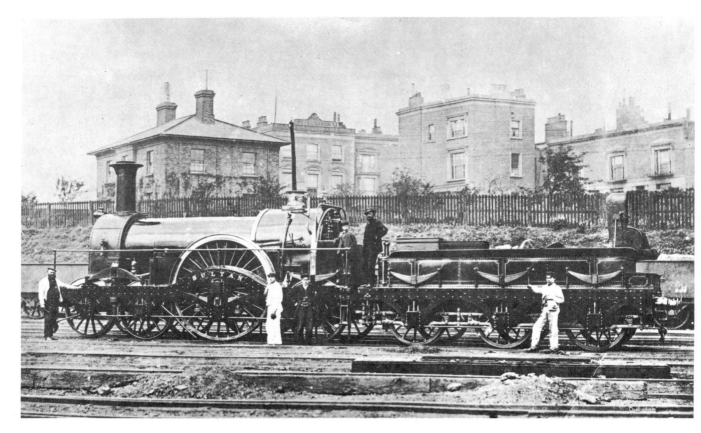

Above *The Sultan, one of six 4–2–2 locomotives built in 1847 at Swindon works for the Great Western Railway. The wood lugging of the boiler and firebox was originally exposed.*

Below *The Vulcan, a broad-gauge locomotive from the age when huge driving wheels were relied upon to produce high speeds on passenger trains.*

Yet for all this the Great Western emerged from the start – as befitted the only British line to preserve its individuality almost unchanged for well over a century – the magnificent achievement of a man who worked 20 hours a day and snatched what rest he could in a strange black caravan of his own devising. It swept up the Thames valley in curves permitting 80-mph speeds, crossed a bridge in which few save its builders had faith, passed through the line's own new town of Swindon and entered the high portal of the Box tunnel, which at nearly two miles was then the world's longest and which created in its building all the anxiety, delay and death characteristic of such works. Only here, as the line dropped down to the Avon gorge and Bath, were the gradients briefly sharpened to 1 in 100, and for most of the distance Brunel was able to restrict them to less than 1 in 1000.

A view of a tunnel portal near Bath on the
Great Western formed the frontispiece of J. C.
Bourne's guide to the line.

Below *Section diagram of a locomotive, published in 1848.*

Bottom *Brunel's Channel-side track near Dawlish, Devon, showing a landslip which took place a few years after the opening of this section.*

Above *A view of the first Munich station, designed by Friedrich Bürklein in 1849.*

Right *A medal commemorating the opening of one of Europe's earliest, most important international rail links, Belgium to the Rhine.*

Opposite top *By the late 1840s, as this view of Florence station, testifies, Italy had established a tradition of grandiose station architecture which was to endure for nearly a century.*

Opposite bottom *A German second-class carriage of 1838. Buffers upholstered in leather or hide were commonly employed in the early days.*

Passenger comforts

AS railroads grew, so did the need for passengers to be housed and fed *en route*. To meet the first demand there sprang up in London, in major provincial cities and at important junctions the earliest caravanserais of a new type, hotels which might be either integrated into the station building or freestanding. But the second problem was less easily solved for the traveler who demanded something more substantial than those pre-packed meals which the railroads from the first provided. Many decades were to pass before the advent of the dining-car (and, similarly, of the corridor giving access to a train-toilet). But with typical journeys such as London/Birmingham or London/Bristol occupying some four hours, the problems of intake and output became as pressing for travelers as for locomotives. To service both, there were hence developed such half-way houses as Swindon, Wolverton and Crewe. Here, trains were halted for 20 minutes or so while lady passengers made a discreet dash for the toilets and their escorts organized the supply of soup, buns, cold chicken and appropriate drinks.

Replica of a first-class British carriage of 1834.

If only because the catering companies held monopoly concessions the cuisine was rarely elegant, and there remains on record a letter from Isambard Brunel himself complaining of the spurious coffee served at Swindon. But the advent of the refreshment room marked a new era in bulk catering, and it has been suggested that the whole concept of bar-drinking and snack-bar eating entered Europe with the coming of the railroads.

All aboard for one of the excursion trains, a special to the races in 1847.

A number of other ancillary services grew up around the young railroads, largely instituted by enterprising nonconformists. By 1840, for instance, George Bradshaw had issued his first timetable and Thomas Cook organized his first excursion. But one facet of these early years has certainly received too scant attention here—the improvement of signaling systems.

This was a subject which excited a good deal of very ill-informed public attention, thanks to the accidents inevitable in forming any new technology. But the story is a complex one, and it is perhaps enough to say here that most of the components of safe control—the use of the electric telegraph, the despatch of trains at "block" intervals (i.e. only when a stretch of line was known to be clear) rather than at timed intervals, and the centralization and interlocking of control levers—were known by the early 1840s. More years were to pass, however, and not a few lives to be lost, before they were so generally adopted that the railroads became the safest as well as the most civilized of all means of travel.

The fixed signals operated by "policemen" or "bobbies" were, in their early days, highly individual in design.

After 1840

BY 1840, only a decade after the opening of the Liverpool & Manchester line, Britain had built over 1500 route-miles of track. In the next five years, though, as much again was to be opened, and construction was to continue at an average rate of some 300 miles a year until about 1880.

With so high a rate of building, this book can mention only a few historic achievements. One such was William Cubitt's South Eastern railroad to Dover, which branched off the Brighton line and drove across Kent on an almost straight course until the white cliffs were reached. Here a sea-wall had to be built and—as an event which was treated as a public spectacle—an entire hill removed with ten tons of gunpowder before the Channel port was reached in 1844.

In building the SER, Cubitt experimented with his own forms of rail and sleeper, for despite the widespread use of Locke's bull-head rail the question of track formation was still an open one. In the Midlands for instance, a former military engineer named Charles Vignoles was favoring a flat-bottomed rail with a section resembling an inverted T. This did not at the time find favor in Britain. But a similar form devised by an American engineer and first rolled in Wales soon became adopted as the norm beyond the Atlantic and the Channel, and flat-bottom rail has now been adopted for British Railways' own standard.

Vignoles is less happily associated with one of the greatest works of this period, the forming of a three-mile bore through the Pennines near Woodhead. 1500 feet above the sea and up to 600 feet below the surface, this tunnel was set in wild and lonely country which added to the difficulties and dangers of a work-force which also had to face hazards ranging from treacherous rock-strata to premature explosions and the threat of cholera. Soon Vignoles was regretting that he had invested his personal fortune in the new line (and pioneer railway engineers often became very rich men, with Robert Stephenson earning the equivalent in modern money of some $1,250,000 per year). Though later in life he was to accumulate a second fortune, Vignoles resigned almost bankrupt from the Woodhead project and saw Joseph Locke appointed in his place.

Considering Locke's distaste for tunneling, this was an ironic outcome of events. But the work was eventually carried through to a successful close, so that by the end of 1845 Britain could add to its impressive list of engineering "firsts" that of the earliest true mountain tunnel.

The Battle of the Gauges

MEANWHILE, in the west, Brunel was busy prolonging the broad-gauge GWR. His eyes were set on the very tip of Cornwall; but the first stage on the route onward from Bristol was Exeter, which he reached before 1845. Further west, the great engineer was soon to be led into that strange and unsuccessful experiment with trains propelled by air pressure which was called the "**atmospheric** caper", but even on the way to Exeter the track was laid in a way which made it clear that Britain's railroads were entering a new phase.

It has been seen that the engineers of Britain's pioneering trunk lines had tried to restrict their gradients to 1 in 250 or so and had regarded a run at 1 in 100 as steep. But the early 1840s witnessed two developments. One was a realization that railroads built to such high standards could not network the country except at ruinous expense. The other was the construction in both America and the mountainous countries of Europe of lines with long stretches at 1 in 75 or steeper which were successfully worked by conventional locomotives.

And so, quite suddenly, the early perfectionism was abandoned. It is true that the short run built in the Midlands at 1 in 37 was a unique anomaly, but in the same period an important branch on the south coast was taken out of Brighton at steeper than 1 in 90. And so there was nothing very remarkable in Brunel's daring to sharpen his Exeter line to 1 in 80 or so for many miles.

Another western development brought to a head a problem which had been impending for some years. In 1844 the GWR reached Gloucester, a city already served on the standard gauge; and there not only did all passengers change trains but freight and luggage had to be transferred. Perhaps the difficulties of the latter operation were a little exaggerated by the standard-gauge companies which were tired of the GWR's independence. But it was clear that, with tracks knitting together all over Britain, two national gauges could no longer be tolerated.

A perhaps jaundiced view of the chaos produced by the gauge-change at Gloucester in the early 1840s.

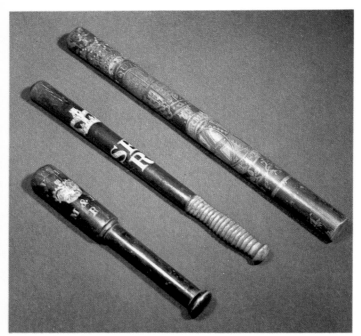

Above (left to right) *Police truncheons of the Manchester & Liverpool and the South Eastern railroads and a signal baton (right) of the London & Birmingham railroad.*

EDINBURGH & GLASGOW RAILWAY.

CAUTION.

JOHN WHITTON, Sailor, belonging to H.M. Ship "Jackall," Charged with being Drunk and Disorderly in the 2 p.m. Train from Edinburgh to Glasgow, on Saturday, the 4th July current, and with Annoying and Assaulting his fellow Passengers. He had to be taken from the Train at Falkirk Station, and was brought before Sheriff SCONCE, and Fined in the Sum of

5 Shillings,
Or Eight Days' Imprisonment.
BY ORDER.

COMPANY'S OFFICES,
GLASGOW, July, 1862.

Warning by example.

*Early timetable for the London & Folkstone
Railway.*

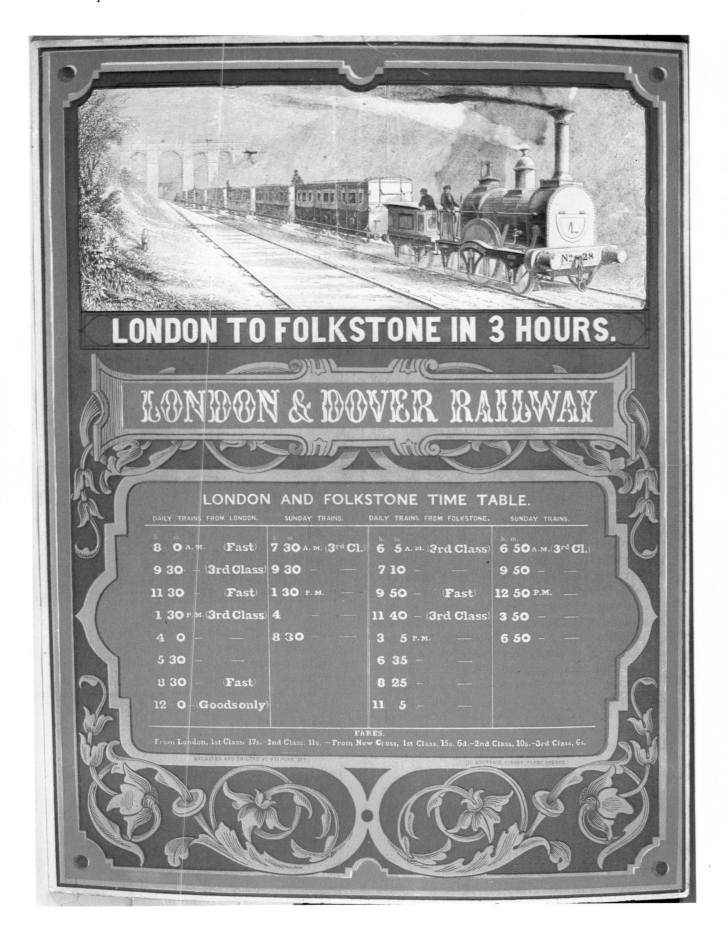

LONDON TO FOLKSTONE IN 3 HOURS.

LONDON & DOVER RAILWAY

LONDON AND FOLKSTONE TIME TABLE.

DAILY TRAINS FROM LONDON.		SUNDAY TRAINS.		DAILY TRAINS FROM FOLKSTONE.		SUNDAY TRAINS.	
h. m.		h. m.		h. m.		h. m.	
8 0 A.M.	(Fast)	7 30 A.M. (3rd Cl.)		6 5 A.M.	(3rd Class)	6 50 A.M. (3rd Cl.)	
9 30 —	(3rd Class)	9 30 —		7 10 —		9 50 —	—
11 30 —	(Fast)	1 30 P.M.	—	9 50 —	(Fast)	12 50 P.M.	—
1 30 P.M.	(3rd Class)	4		11 40 —	(3rd Class)	3 50 —	—
4 0 —	—	8 30 —		3 5 P.M.		6 50 —	—
5 30 —	—			6 35 —			
8 30 —	(Fast)			8 25 —			
12 0 —	(Goods only)			11 5 —			

FARES.
From London, 1st Class, 17s.—2nd Class, 11s.—From New Cross, 1st Class, 15s. 6d.—2nd Class, 10s.—3rd Class, 6s.

ENGRAVED AND PRINTED BY STEPHEN SLY,   11, BOUVERIE STREET, FLEET STREET.

Government steps in

THE British railroad network, more than that of any other country, grew up through uncoordinated private enterprise. In its earliest days there had certainly been those who called for some kind of national supervision. But after a decade or two the system seemed to be operating so well that the average Briton preferred his wastefully-duplicated routes and his company wars (which more than once led to dramatic physical violence) to the bureaucratically-planned, monopolistic schemes of continental Europe.

From time to time, however (for instance, to settle the debate as to the best route to Brighton), the government had stepped in, and in 1844 Gladstone had steered through a reluctant assembly a Regulating Act which standardized a number of railroad matters and even assumed the right of nationalization in an emergency. This new battle of the gauges provided a clear case for such state intervention, and so after a stirring series of comparative races the GWR was forbidden to extend its broad-gauge metals further into the Midlands.

These mid-decade years were climacteric in another way, for during the period a fury of speculation in what was virtually the only outlet for risk capital was followed by the in-

evitable market crash—and one which spotlighted not a little sharp practice. The number of bankruptcies ensuing has, perhaps, been exaggerated, but certainly for a few years after 1846 British railway construction proceeded more cautiously than before. It did so now, however, with the most lofty blessing; for in 1842 (and in a carriage equipped with a special signal to order the driver to slow down), Queen Victoria had been at last persuaded to travel by train.

Three examples of the cartoonist's wit of the period of the railroad boom in Britain.

Stocktaking

BY the middle 1840s, British railway technology had reached almost a point of rest. At that time, men could look forward to the great civil engineering achievements which awaited in the near future, the most notable of which were to be the opening of routes from London to Scotland and through North Wales to Holyhead for Dublin. Here, as if to epitomize two contrasting styles of railroad construction, the Irish and one of the Scottish routes used typically Stephensonian sea-level surveys which avoided hill-climbing at the expense of some notable bridges over river estuaries, while the other route to Scotland (by Locke) offered more direct access but involved long, tough climbs over the Border hills.

Alternatively, men could cast a backward glance to marvel at what had been done in those few years since the first trunk routes had been opened and Britain had entered fully into the railroad age. Here it was only in one department that there was little to show—that of the design of locomotives and rolling stock.

The early 1840s had certainly seen a general enlargement of locomotives (so that six, rather than four, wheels became the norm), a cleaning-up of design, and improvements in such matters as valve gear. But major developments had been held back by a red herring characteristic of early railroad history. This time the villain was the belief that it was essential to keep the center of gravity of engines very low, the extreme of this school of thought being reached by Thomas Crampton with his huge driving wheels set behind the firebox.

Similarly, there had been little change in rolling stock since the days of the Liverpool & Manchester line. Some specialized forms of freight car had been developed to cope with the variety of goods which the railroads now carried—not least for the handling of Her Majesty's mails—and for first-class passengers there were available a few saloon coaches and primitive sleeping-cars. But even these were badly sprung and supported on two rigid axles, and second-class British passengers still traveled, as often as not, in ill-upholstered, badly lit and inadequately braked vehicles little removed from cattle-trucks. As for the third-class passenger, it was not until after the passing of the 1844 Act that he could expect even a roof over his head.

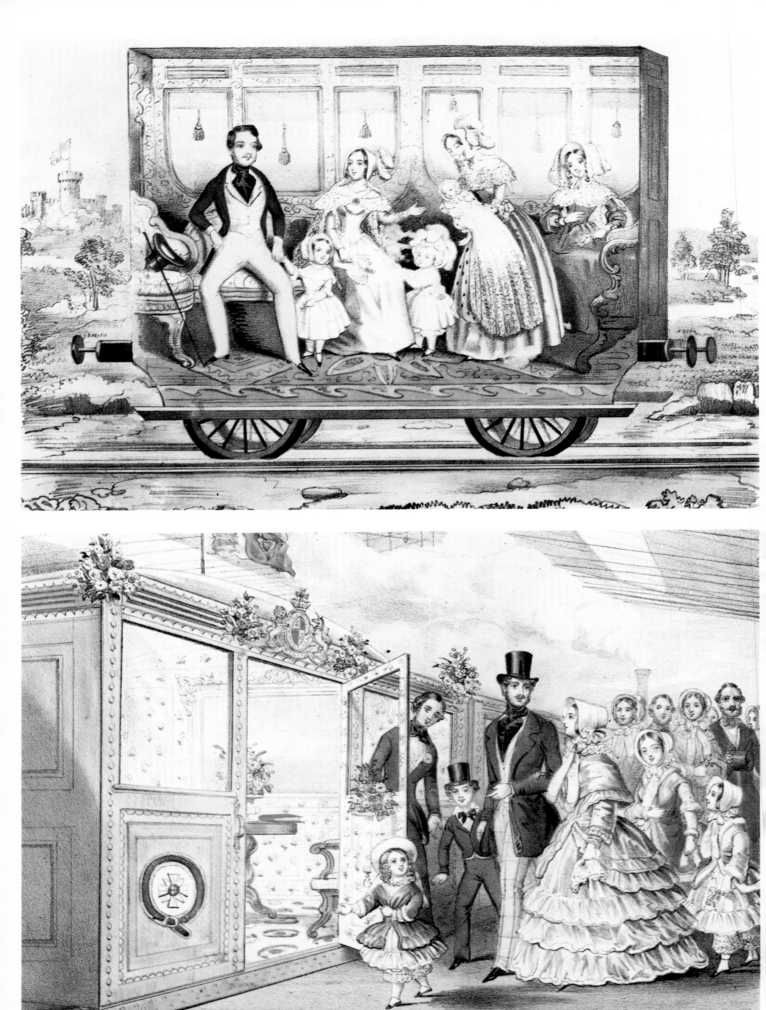

The comparative luxury enjoyed by the Royal Family in their first rail journeys to Scotland (opposite top and bottom) contrasts with (top) the more plebeian conditions depicted in the "Five-a-side" carriage.

Above *Early passenger accommodation at its crudest – the interior of a third-class carriage on the Stockton & Darlington line.*

Right *Symbol of royalty: the rear lamp used on early royal trains.*

Josiah Stickney, built in the 1850s, epitomizes the American school at its most characteristic and with its own elegance.

Years of Expansion

IN 1848 Britain's building program gathered full momentum again to show between 5000 and 6000 miles of track—about a third of the length which was ever to be built there. In America, by contrast, the 1848 figure of around 8000 miles represented only one thirtieth of a peak of nearly a quarter of a million miles—almost one-third of the world's total, but serving a nation with only about a twentieth of the world's population and a still lower proportion of the world's area. The achievement of such a mileage, it should be noted, was made possible largely by the grants of public money and land which had also characterized American canal construction, for American governments had favored investment in these two media rather than in roads.

This quantitative contrast alone gives reason to carry the story of American railroad construction forward for a few more decades. For some years after the first laying down of tracks from Baltimore, then, enterprise had been restricted to the eastern seaboard. But there (and despite opposition from reactionaries with the suggestion that railroads were in some sense private and hence undemocratic), city after city swiftly became the nucleus of a rail system, so that by 1833 one could travel the 190 miles between New York City and Baltimore and two years later Boston could boast of three separate roads. One of these was shortly to begin work on the 4½-mile Hoosac tunnel, and as a comment on the difficulties which America encountered with substantial engineering works it is worth noting that this, though little longer than some British tunnels of the 1840s, was not to be

The Baltimore & Ohio railroad had a tradition of substantial architecture. This is the brownstone station of 1852 in Washington, D.C.

Suspension bridges were mistrusted in European railroad practice. The most famous early American example is this, near the Niagara Falls.

An early American poster.

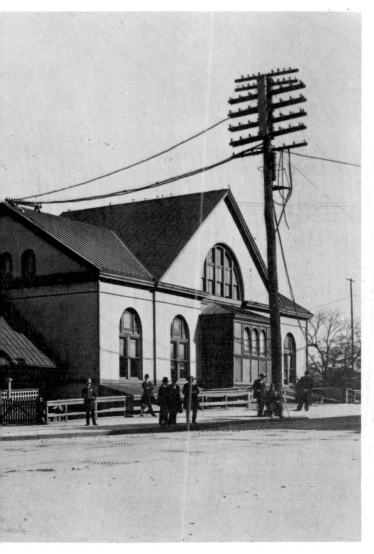

completed until 1875. It was not until well into the twentieth century that America could show any tunnels remotely comparable to such European giants as the Mont Cenis.

But—once again—these comparatively light railroads could be built fast, and before 1840 most of the east coast from the border to Georgia was rail-linked and America was constructing lines faster than the whole of Europe combined. What may be even more significant is that, of the 26 states which composed the Union in that year, only four lacked some kind of railroad. The lines were reaching inland now to Ohio, Kentucky, Indiana and the Great Lakes, carrying the manufactured goods of Europe to the hinterland of America and, in return, bearing away the rich foodstuffs which lay beyond the coastal mountains. Not surprisingly, freight traffic proved much more important than passenger movements on most American roads, whereas in Europe the balance was fairly equal. Nor was it only the commerce of the sixty-year-old republic which benefited from the coming of the railroads, for their construction provided work for the Irish escaping from the famines of the 1840s and for Europeans seeking a new life. The greatest sufferers in this age were the men associated with inland navigation, who now saw their trade decline as had their British counterparts a decade before.

By 1850, America could display a network of lines covering every state east of the Mississippi from Maine to Georgia. And, just as the tracks themselves had knit together, so the local companies were starting to fuse into such substantial joint enterprises as the New York Central and the Pennsylvania Railroad.

Towards the Far West

EVEN the 1000-mile run from New York to Chicago, long as it was by European standards, dwindled to almost commuter scale when measured against a dream which had occurred to Asa Whitney and others as far back as the mid-40s and began to dominate men of vision in the 1850s. As yet there was little of civilization or even population in the far West outside California, and still less of it in the huge and lawless hinterlands between the Mississippi valley and the Rockies. But the frontier was creeping onward, and many believed that the swiftest and surest way to speed its movement would be to create at least one railroad (other than the little Panama line eventually opened in 1855) which should span the continent from the Atlantic to the Pacific and act as iron spine to the nation. Whitney himself was even prepared to undertake its construction as a private enterprise, but his ambitions were rather more practical than those of a rival who envisaged a railroad built to a 10-foot gauge whose carriages should be "moving palaces, . . . 200 feet in length."

Inevitably, there was jealous discussion as to which city should form the eastern terminal of such a transcontinental line, though Chicago seemed to have the strongest claims. Inevitably, too, the desirable degree of public involvement became a matter of contention. In 1853 Congress commissioned a survey of four possible routes, but debates dragged on and before the matter was resolved America became engulfed in economic difficulties. These in turn were followed by the Civil War.

The conflict proved ruinous to many aspects of American life, particularly in the South. But since the railroads continued for the most part to be run on normal commercial lines, those of the North, at least, were revitalized. This was due largely to the fact that, from Abraham Lincoln downwards, the Union leaders appreciated the contribution which efficient transport could make to victory.

And the northern railroads justified this trust. Tens of thousands of men were shifted at a rate which commanders had never witnessed before, special military lines were opened where necessary with their bridges supported (in Lincoln's own words) on "bean-poles and corn-stalks," and there was enough spare capacity to permit trade with Europe to continue and hence for vital support to flow in. The Confederate forces, too, began by

making considerable use of their scantier railroads; but the South lacked the means and the discipline to keep these in repair and had to cannibalize equipment to such an extent that its own actions, as much as those of the enemy, were responsible for the destruction of well over half its rail resources by the time hostilities ended. The part played by railroads throughout the war is forever epitomized by the militarily minor incident of the Andrews raid, with its dramatic chase by train and linesman's trolley to the key railroad junction of Chattanooga.

Even while the battles raged, though, Lincoln was looking ahead. Peace might bring a true union of the states; but they would be impoverished and anxious for trade with Asia as well as with Europe, in need of better communications, and demanding of a physical expression that here was one great nation. Above all, once North and South were at peace there must be no danger of new secessionist movements in the Far West. Though even Lincoln did not appreciate how swift the changes which it brought were to be, it was clear that nothing could fulfill all those ends better than the building of the long-mooted transcontinental railroad.

The Golden Spike

IT was early in the 1863–64 session of Congress, after a final dispute concerning the gauge had been settled, that the high-ball signal was at last given for America's first transcontinental line. This project was to be operated by commercial companies with shares made available to the public, but it would also rely on substantial government backing which, by being linked to the land-grant system, would also encourage settlement.

Effectively, Chicago had won the battle to be the eastern terminal, though the new tracks of the Union Pacific railroad in fact branched off that company's existing network at Omaha on the border of Iowa and Nebraska. In the west, the Central Pacific company set out simultaneously from Sacramento. The exact meeting point of the two systems was left to destiny and to the efforts of the two labor forces, themselves recruited from the usual mixture of nationalities in the East, a strong Asiatic contingent in the West, and freed slaves and demobilized men from the Civil War to reinforce both parties.

73

It should perhaps be mentioned here that they might be reinforced in another way, for in this period power tools were beginning to come to the aid of the railway-builder. Already the first pneumatic drills had been devised and already too – for those prepared to face its hazards – nitroglycerin was available to replace black powder. But these aids played little part in the construction of the first transcontinental line itself, which owed far more to the muscle-power of men like the legendary John Henry.

So, at the close of 1863, the two spearheads thrust out to conquer mountains and deserts. There was opposition in the form of Sioux raids, not only in the years of building but in those of operation, but perhaps greater courage was needed to overcome the baking heat of five desert summers and the blizzard cold of the winters between. On the debit side of an heroic story was a pervading smell of corruption associated with much of the contracting, and the skimped work inevitable when subsidies were paid by the mile.

Once the western party had hacked through snowdrifts to cross the huge obstacle of the Sierras, indeed, construction became an out-and-out race, with bets being laid – and lost – as the parties challenged each other to lay 5, 7 or 10 miles a day. Not surprisingly, much of this work had to be redone before the tracks could be regarded as fit to carry heavy cars on their week-long coast-to-coast hauls. And when eventually (and slightly out of alignment) the two teams reached the same longitude, building was going ahead so fast that the advance parties slipped past each other.

This small matter was soon rectified, however; and on May 10, 1869, after a long wait by the official western party, the scene was set for the formal linking of the two sections. Promontory Point, Utah, then witnessed the completion of the nearly 1800 miles of track which at the time formed the world's longest railroad. At the third attempt the directors managed to hit the celebratory golden spike, which was immediately pulled up again and replaced with a more serviceable fixture.

As the spike was banged into the laurel cross-tie, a telegraph impulse flashed across the nation, and was directly linked not only to a signal above the Capitol in Washington but to the bell-towers of a hundred village churches. Cannon crashed, a four-mile parade set off in Chicago, and in San Francisco the city fire-bells rang out in chorus. The United States were united at last.

American Carriages

MANY of those factors which distinguished travel in the New World – the great distances and comparatively low speeds which made day-long journeys common, the uneven and sharply-curved tracks, and not least the spacious loading gauges – combined to produce one final characteristic of American as opposed to European railroading. This was the accent placed on roominess and comparative comfort in passenger rolling-stock. It was present from almost the first years and could be noted in even the cheapest accommodation – for the elaborate class distinctions favored by most European railroad companies found little place in their American counterparts.

The first consideration was that, on the average bumpy American railroad, a journey of more than suburban distance would have been intolerably uncomfortable in the type

of four-wheeled boxcar-with-benches which was all that British companies offered their penny-a-mile passengers. Hence America had had to replace fixed axles with bogies in the interest of smoother riding alone. But to make economic use of these expensive underparts it was desirable that the coaches should accommodate plenty of passengers, and so during the 1830s American roads began to boast vehicles about sixty feet in length – giants whose like were not to be seen in Europe for several decades.

These coaches were also better-sprung and better-coupled than their British counterparts. They were warmed by stoves at a time when even an English aristocrat had to cling to a hot-water bottle, lit at night by lamps which, if not brilliant, were superior to their transatlantic equivalents, and so generously glazed that one example appeared to the ever-observant Fanny Kemble as "a long greenhouse upon wheels." Soon after 1840, all that the average American coach lacked by modern standards were toilet facilities, flexible "vestibule" connections between cars, and (most important) one of the continuous braking systems which allowed a 1000-ton train to be handled as a single unit. When these devices entered general railroad practice later in the century they were to be introduced mainly from America, though such other features of American rolling-stock as the **clerestory** roof and the open end-platform were rather less commonly met with outside their homeland.

Yet to European eyes the most striking feature of all in early American cars was their open planning, with seats arranged on each side of a central aisle. Whereas in Europe (and not only in England, for the French were equally jealous of personal or family privacy) the compartment type of carriage remained normal even after the coming of corridors, those companies such as the Mohawk & Hudson which experimented with a "multiple stage-coach" form of first-class design found it unpopular, and even the deliciously elegant "Surrey with a fringe on top" double-deckers had few imitators. By fortunate coincidence, the long and open-planned type of car suggested by technical considerations was also that most socially acceptable in a pioneering and democratic mid-century America.

An early Pullman car. Note the fold-down bunks, oil lamps, spittoons and wicker seats arranged on either side of the center aisle.

1859 saw George M. Pullman's sleeping-cars operating in Canada. In this type there was no need for conversion from day to night usage.

The Coming of Luxury

THE American passenger of the 1850s could hence travel by day in considerably more ease than his European counterpart, class for class. Some coaches were even provided with those prerequisites of homely American comfort, rocking chairs. But as more and more cities of the hinterland increased in their agricultural, manufacturing and commercial importance, even before the opening of the transcontinental route, night travel became unavoidable. In both Europe and America there had been early experiments with various primitive types of *couchette* offering some type of horizontal accommodation to the overnight traveler, and in addition, Europe had built a few bedrooms-on-wheels for its monarchs, while America had a tradition of state-rooms on its inland navigation routes. But before 1860 the time had come when conditions of American rail travel demanded proper sleeping-cars to be at the disposal of the ordinary traveler.

This idea occurred almost simultaneously to several men. But the most famous of them, the one whose name was eventually to become a synonym for comfort and luxury, was George Mortimer Pullman. Born in New York State in 1831, Pullman had by the early 1850s set up as a builder and engineer in fast-expanding Chicago; and there, in 1858, he converted two cars of the Chicago & Alton railroad into vehicles which, though still at one remove from the custom-built sleeping-car, provided prototypes for the carriage produced when Pullman returned to this field of invention in 1864. This carriage was the 16-wheeler *Pioneer*, a vehicle so grand that it was chartered for Lincoln's funeral. Four years later, the Pullman company supplied the world's first regular dining car to a Canadian railroad.

Shortly afterwards, such comforts were to cross the Atlantic. The story here is complex, for though the name of Pullman became familiar in Britain from the 1870s onwards it was not he but one of his rivals, the disreputable Colonel William d'Alton Mann, who teamed up with Georges Nagelmackers of Belgium in the founding years of the great and international *Wagons-Lits* company of continental Europe. Furthermore, the design favored in Europe for what Mark Twain described as "that culmination of all charity and human kindness, a sleeping car" differed considerably from the American pattern. But few would dispute that the concept of real comfort on wheels, by day and by night, was the greatest of all America's gifts to the railroad age.

The Second Half of the Century

THE completion of the Union Pacific/ Central Pacific link had not, of course, marked the end of the heroic era of American railroad construction but rather its beginning. Even while the first line was being built another was started and before a further fifty years has passed five more such links in the United States and two in Canada had been opened. A precedent, too, had been set for similar immense lines spanning the full breadth of Australia, networking India and penetrating deep into China and South Africa. Not least, the closing of the century saw the ownership of the world's longest railroad revert to the Old World with the completion of the 7000-mile Trans-Siberian railroad.

Today, when concrete has for many purposes taken over from steel as steel took over from iron a century back, the age of railroad construction has still not ended. It is true that in Europe it was drawing to a close even by 1870, and that a golden period of utilization before the first World War was to be followed by one of closures. The USA, too, seemed to be rail-saturated by 1920. But new railroads are still being planned in Central Africa, China, Canada, the Middle East and elsewhere, with the accent usually on freight carriage.

In general, though, the story of the world's railroads since 1870—and, even more, since 1900—lies less in physical expansion than in new techniques. A century ago, the railroad arts had changed comparatively little since the age of Robert Stephenson forty years earlier: even in the locomotive department, Britain still relied for its passenger-express racers on designs with a single pair of huge driving wheels and America on the slower and more powerful four-coupled engine. But the public was beginning to demand better trains and the first years of the 1900s hence saw the appearance of those new breeds—notably the "Pacific" or 4–6–2—which with such technical refinements as super-heating were to predominate in almost every major country in the first half of the twentieth century.

Similar changes took place in freight haulage; but for the ordinary traveler the most conspicuous advance in the years after 1870 was in the improvement of passenger rolling-stock. Steadily, over half a century, the all-steel bogie carriage—bellows-connected and continuously-braked, electrically-lit and steam-heated—was assembled from developments in both America and Europe, while sleeping-and dining-cars, buffets and saloons and specialized luxury services could be found on all the world's great expresses. Up to the late 1920s long-distance railroad travel was an unchallenged feature of a way of life, whether offered by commercial companies as in the United States or by the state authorities which increasingly administered the tracks elsewhere.

But already the automobile, the air-liner and the motor-bus or coach were making their challenges felt. With such exceptions as an increased reliance on diesel and electric traction and an outburst of main-line racing in the mid-1930s, the world's railroads were slow to adapt to a new age. Not until some years after World War II, indeed, was the need appreciated for a reassessment of the place of railroads in the second half of a troubled century.

Today, though, there are signs on many fronts of a railroad renaissance. The rural

A well-known scene showing the rescue of a train snowbound in New England in the late 1860s.

branch-line certainly seems doomed, but in a world increasingly conscious of environmental considerations the suburban-commuter and long-distance freight services cannot reasonably be challenged in their fields. The revivified passenger express, triumphant in Japan, has found supporters even in an America which seemed oversold on air transport. And in support of the rail services of today and tomorrow all the devices of modern technology are being put to work in fields ranging from track maintenance to computerized marshaling.

The railroad still offers—as it and its predecessor the tramway have done for over 400 and perhaps over 4000 years—the most economic form of land transport in terms of manpower and horse-power. It is modest, for instance, even in its demands on increasingly-scarce forms of fuel. Still more important, in a crowded and chaotic world, may be the fact that its movements are uniquely safe, disciplined and suited to automation. And so most certainly, whatever the future may bring by way of new track formations and tractive systems, the end is not yet in sight for a device which was well-tested even before Stephenson steamed out of Liverpool or the first locomotives left Baltimore.

This six-coupled engine presumably hauled heavier loads through Nebraska than the single composite coach shown here.

Right *"Lightning"* expresses of the Erie railroad in the 1870s, when the system still used a broad gauge.

Bottom *American passenger rolling-stock around 1870. Note the "clerestory" roof, the open end platforms and the ornateness of the chimney from the heating stove.*